Evolving

A Spiritual Guide for Living

By

Michael C. Fikaris

ISBN: 1-4033-3981-3 (e-book)
ISBN: 1-4033-3982-1 (Paperback)

This book is printed on acid free paper.

AuthorHouse – rev. 02/20/07

DEDICATION

Thanks to the many Teachers throughout my life!
Especially to Bill Duby, Angela Silva, and to my wife
Cecilia,
all of whom had a most profound effect upon my
consciousness.

In addition, I would like to credit the following people
for their Divine guidence and help along the way:
My parents, Michael C. Lekas, Marc Raymont,
Roy Masters, Gladys Lobos and all my children.

I love you all!

iv

TABLE OF CONTENTS

INTRODUCTION

Just the fact that you've delved this far in your investigation of this book, are now reading even the first sentence of it's introduction, speaks volumes about you:

Primarily, it says you're considering – maybe even hoping? - that something you need will be found within its pages. And we both know you didn't just stumble upon a book about how to spiritualize no less than every aspect of your life while looking for some light reading. No, we are here together because you're looking for answers. Good, because that's what Michael Fikaris' book provides.

Secondarily it says that you're not someone who's interested in a book containing three or four spiritual truths repeated fifteen different ways over three hundred pages.

Nope.

It reveals you to be the type of person who says, "Give it to me now, all of it – I can take it".

Good again, because this book will do just that: give it to you straight, without the airy-fairy rainbows and halos... not that there's anything wrong with that. Everyone learns at their own rate, in whatever format they require, to 'get' whatever it is that they need. This is why there are hundreds of spiritual teachings the world over that say basically the same thing in hundreds of different ways. You're here because the way you want it is straight-forward and complete.

There are no accidents. You came to the right place. You're exactly where you belong, ready for some answers.

A popular lament among mothers and fathers says, "When you become a parent, nobody gives you a handbook on how to properly raise your children". And however unfair this may seem, it's true. But what if the priceless information everyone seems to need regarding child-rearing could be learned *before* the gift of parenthood. *Just maybe, if everyone knew how to raise, to nurture, to correct and love **themselves** first,* there might be far less of a global clamoring for some unwritten guide instructing us in the proper ways to parent our offspring.

This is exactly what Evolving is: A handbook instructing you, the 'give it to me now – I can take it' reader in the correct way to raise yourself. It's about how to care for yourself on the spiritual, mental/emotional and physical levels. It's about healing and freeing yourself of the bad dreams you've created and keep trying to wake up from. It's about fearlessly taking responsibility for yourself, and in the process, becoming the You you know you truly are.

Evolving is not a book of easy suggestions and luke-warm encouragement – it is a book of challenges designed to arouse and strengthen and free. I *dare* you to meet the challenges this book offers. I'm sure you can... that's why you're here.

Randall Alden
Stockholm, Sweden 2002

FOREWORD

What are you searching for? It is incredible how many different religions, systems and teachings there are today in the world. You can find countless techniques and concepts throughout the world to heal anything that you can imagine. And many people spend a lot of time, energy and money investigating numerous teachings. Consequently, the individual acquires a lot of knowledge, but his/her life improves very little - if at all. The reason for this is quite simple: Knowledge is not the solution to your problems. What you do with the knowledge can become the solution. Understand that it is not what you know, it is what you do.

The most profound truths are easily understood intellectually, but for most, very difficult to put into practice. People read book after book, listen to endless tapes and run the lecture circuit to receive the same information over and over and over again. Each time they hear the same thing a little differently, they suddenly get a rush of excitement (false enthusiasm) and believe that they have just had a great revelation. Soon, like usual, the new information becomes old news and the search continues. Why? Simple. The information was never actually put into practice.

Knowledge without practical application is useless. It is not only useless, it is also dangerous. Knowing the truth and not living the truth can be a living hell. Knowledge does not become real until it is applied in the body through action. There are many steps that one must take to spiritual enlightenment. Accumulation of knowledge is one of the steps, but in reality it is the least important. Knowledge can be power only if it is put into practice. Living the life, (not knowing the life), will bring true happiness and ultimately true mastery.

In working towards your goal of enlightenment, it is important to train in a practical down to earth manner. Don't waste your time with thirty different ways to heal depression. Find one that you like and practice it until you've mastered it. Then take your next step and master that. When one thing is mastered, then all things are possible. You cannot become a basketball star by reading a book or hearing lectures from basketball experts or by watching games. You must actually go out and practice and then play the game. Well the same holds true for life. Stop spinning your wheels and searching for what you already have and play the game! Or, as it is said, "Just do it!" It is my hope that this book aids you in the practical application of your spiritual gifts.

Michael

Chapter One

SPIRITUALITY

In this day and age there is a lot happening that many are consciously unaware of. There is a whole NEW AGE upon us and most people have no idea that this world is actually changing. Not changing in the sense that everything is in constant change, but changing in the sense of total revolution. The events in Europe during the 90's and within the Eastern Block indicate very strongly that things on this planet are changing. Many people mistakenly believed that "these ARE the changes". That was only the very beginning, which is now very evident. But what has happened in the world in recent history is also really just the beginning of startling events that will transpire in the years to come to approximately the year 2030. In the meantime, be aware that every aspect of life will very soon be much different than the way we were raised to know it.

More importantly, at this time, there is a spiritual revolution of great proportions. Millions of people around the world are suddenly, since the early eighties turning to spirituality. Not religion, not to the established old-line churches, but to the purer teachings. In fact, since that time, churches such as the Catholic, Orthodox and Jewish faiths have suffered great losses in their congregations. Yet more people than ever are turning to spirituality, and this continues to increase steadily.

People everywhere are searching. Searching for God, inner peace, or just something that they really aren't sure of. This search is apparent in today's society with popularity not only in psychics, astrologers and spirituality, but also in the field of Psychology, self-improvement workshops and the continual attraction to higher education. But why the search? What is it that has been lost or missing? If people are searching for something, they must have lost something or are missing something. They know it is there somewhere, but they just can't quite put their finger on it. Way down deep in all human beings is an urge, a very subtle urge, yet an urge that is unmistakably present. An urge that is with us throughout each and every incarnation. An urge that we carry to our death bed. And then upon transition, as we stand over our body and watch it turn blue and gag and choke and struggle for life, we realize that we have missed something very important...

What is it that people keep missing? What are people today constantly searching for? Love? Happiness? Companionship? Peace? Joy? Health? Fulfillment? Wisdom? Wealth? Self-realization? God? Whether your search includes some or all of these things, success is nearly at hand. There is an old story of the creation of mankind, (who often is not very kind at all). The Creator was with three of His Archangels and He asked, "Where should we put the soul of man? We must put it in a place where it can be found, but it must be searched for, so that man can appreciate himself and all of his abilities and powers. And it must not be found accidentally, his soul must be sought out, so that only the truly sincere will attain the treasures of heaven." So the first Angel said "Let us put man's soul at the bottom of the oceans. Surely they will not easily find it there." And the Lord said, "No, someday man will reach the bottom of My oceans and his soul will be too easily obtained." And the second Angel said, "Let us put man's soul in the deepest reaches of outer space. Surely he would not easily find it there." And the Lord said, "No, for someday man will reach out into the farthest reaches of space and there he would accidentally find his soul." So the third and wisest of the Angels said, "Lord, hide man's soul within his own body, for he will never look there for it." And so it was done! And even to this day, men and women are searching and searching for that something that is missing in their lives. And they are still looking everywhere - everywhere but within... That elusive something that is missing from our modern day lives that keeps nagging at us way back in the deepest part of our minds, is our very own soul.

Yet in the world in which we live, most everything pulls our attention outside of ourselves. "What if a man gained the whole world and lost his own soul?", asked Jesus. Well, the "What if" has come true! Man has gained the whole world and in the process has lost the only thing of value to his existence. With television, job careers, money and worldly power, maybe two percent of the entire world are truly connected. The other ninety-eight percent are doing little or nothing for their spiritual life. This does not mean that you must give up anything at all. All you must do is become aware.

Spiritually unfolding is a process of becoming more and more aware. For example, at some point in time you became aware that maybe you were a little different than most. Then at another point in time you may have become aware of energy, your aura, your chakras, ...etc. So in the process of unfolding your spirituality, or your spiritual gifts, (clairvoyance, psychometry, precognition, telepathy, ...and so on), you become more and more aware. Aware of what? Aware of you! You are what you are searching for. But to find something, you must have the ability to SEE. Therefore, as you develop your clairvoyance (clear seeing), you begin to see yourself more and more clearly for probably the first time.

Michael C. Fikaris

Before you took that body, you were a living being. A vortex of energy within a "Light Body". You were not just energy, but intelligent energy. Energy that had consciousness, identity and purpose. You took one third of you (your energy), and co-created a physical body, another third to co-create mental and emotional bodies. So who are you really: that which you have co-created, or that which is the co-creator? If you took some clay and formed a clay statue, do you think of yourself as the statue? Of course not! Yet most people think of themselves as their body, or their mind or even their profession: "I am a Doctor; I am a Lawyer; I am a Teacher; I am a liberal; I am sick; I am tired; I am only human." To hear people identify themselves in these terms is very amusing to me. Especially when they try to convince me or themselves that they are "only human". You are more than human, you are spirit. Now if we could only learn to be humane to ourselves and others, then being human or a human being could take on a whole new meaning... But in reality, we are all spiritual beings.

As you spiritually unfold, or open up to the true spiritual you, you will become more and more aware of how inhumane society really is. And through this new awareness, you will repent, or rethink and then radically change your ways as the fog is lifted from your eyes and you begin to see clearly who you really are. The main problem with people on this planet is an identity crisis. If people knew who they were talking to, and living with, and working with, this world would be a very different place. Well, this self-realization is just around the corner.

More people than ever are searching for that something that is missing from their lives. Their true self is what they long for, and as we individually wake up one by one, we raise the consciousness of the planet just a little bit at a time. Thereby creating a domino effect. Each of us is intertwined with the others. Many are waiting for you to wake up so that they too can awaken unto their true self. Becoming aware of who you are and what it is that you are destined to do in this world and in the next is the precise reason that you have incarnated on this planet. Self-Realization is the required step before God Realization. A true Master is one who is a Self Realized spirit dwelling consciously in this three dimensional world and in the spiritual world simultaneously and has effectively mastered his/her own space and life.

Chapter Two

CHURCH SLEEP

I was raised in one of the "established" churches of the world. My family and all the generations before ours faithfully attended the Greek Orthodox Church. For those of you who are unfamiliar with this particular faith, it is very much like the Catholic Church. There are a few key differences, but these differences are far outnumbered by the similarities. I am also quite familiar with the Catholic Church because I spent four years in Catholic schools in which we were obligated to study that religion on a daily basis, plus attend mass at least three mornings a week. As a member of the Greek Orthodox Church, I served as an alter boy for many years and attended church service faithfully into my mid twenties. I even wanted, as a young boy, to become a priest of that faith.

I had the inner urge many times in my life, but I could not quite see the value of what was happening in what was probably the two of the biggest churches of that time. I was acutely aware that most of the people in church were not really paying attention to what was going on during the service. I found that this fact irritated me greatly. Why would these people keep coming to church every Sunday and not pay attention to what was going on? Then suddenly, one Sunday during church service, I realized that I wasn't paying attention either! I too was there watching everyone else watching everyone else! The pain of my apparent hypocrisy was nearly overwhelming, but that pain was quickly eased as I put a few extra dollars into the donation plate.

But regardless of my feeble attempt to correct my ways by donating money, (which is one of the most popular ways of easing one's conscience in many churches), I was determined to sit through a church service and pay attention. I did not think at the time that this would be such a difficult task. But I soon discovered that this ambition was almost beyond my abilities. Each week I would do a little better until finally I reached a space where I could actually pay attention to the service throughout the entire service. After a few weeks of focusing on the service, I realized that it was almost the same every week. As a matter of fact, it was the exact same words every week except for two parts, the Gospel reading and the sermon.

The sermon was often quite good, but that of course depended upon the priest and was often a little too political. I really believed that the Gospels were good too, but who could understand them? If they didn't read them in Greek or Latin, then they would sing every other sentence with someone else echoing it in the background! And no one knew exactly who or where he was. It was just some faceless voice chiming in from time to time… And then, as if that wasn't difficult enough, they would only give a couple of verses of the Gospel out of context with no interpretation, explanation or even telling you how the story turns out… Well, I thought to myself, this is very interesting. But, people in those religions are not supposed to think intelligently about spirituality or religion, so I let all that go for the time being.

But then, I couldn't help to notice that the priest was doing a lot of things up there at the alter that we weren't aware of. Many times he would turn his back to the congregation and do and say things. Now as an alter boy I was standing right there in front of him, but I could never quite catch what he said or even figure out what he did.

7

Michael C. Fikaris

Plus, by the time I was in my early to mid twenties I couldn't remember everything that I had witnessed as an alter boy.

All in all, what I came to realize back in those days was that there was very little that was comprehensible to me in the entire one hour and forty-five minute church service. Oh sure, I'll admit that when we said the Lord's Prayer I knew the words all right. I didn't understand them, but like everyone else I recited it word for word as if in some zombie-like hypnotic state of consciousness, verbalizing words that were totally meaningless to me at the time. It is amazing to me that with four years in Catholic School, and most of my childhood, (up to age seventeen), going to Sunday School, that not once was the meaning of the Lord's Prayer ever revealed, discussed, or even mentioned. We were forced to commit this prayer and of course the church creed, to memory, given absolutely no understanding whatsoever to the most important prayer given in the Bible.

At one point, I thought I could read the Bible to gain insight into spiritual things. So, every night I would open my Bible and read. I was faithful to this ritual for about three months. After three months, I found myself almost at the end of the first page of the first chapter of the Book of Genesis. Every time I began to read, I would either fall asleep or I would read a whole page and remember nothing of what I had just read. It was if I had left the room while I read the page. So each night I would start over again, until one day I realized that whatever is in there, it must be too deep for me to understand, and I gave it up. I learned later in life that it is not the context of the Bible that puts people to sleep, it is the energy and programming around it that is designed to keep us from understanding it that makes it so difficult. Eventually, at the recommendation of my Teacher, I carried my Bible with me everywhere for about a year. I

8

had it in restaurants, in the bathroom, at the grocery store, in bars, in court... Everywhere. By the end of that year, I could finally read through with ease and understanding.

So anyway, in short, as a young adult, who spent all of his life in churches, I came to realize that I knew nothing of what spirituality or religion was about... And with that knowledge, I knew more than the others. Because they didn't even know that they didn't know.

The large masses of people are programmed and lulled to sleep. They are told not to question or seek for knowledge. Hypnotized into believing that a priest is someone special, chosen as a go-between for man and God. (As if we need someone outside of ourselves to communicate to God!) In both churches I was taught that when I committed a sin, that God was watching and listening, yet I had to go to a priest so that he could ask God for my forgiveness. What? God could only hear me when I cuss and not when I ask for forgiveness? How absurd I thought. But oh yes, intelligent thought is not allowed in Christianity or in most of the other religions.

As I became more awake and aware, I broke through the programming and had probably one of the most important realizations of all concerning the established churches of the world. And I am not just talking about the Greek Orthodox or Catholic Churches, but the majority of the "old world" churches. This realization was so simple, yet so difficult to attain. So difficult because I had never experienced anything other than what I was raised with. So difficult because no one I knew had any real spiritual knowledge to validate what I suspected. So difficult because I felt all alone in a church full of people - and that was frightening. But then I met a spiritual Teacher and all that changed and the reason it changed is in this sentence. I met a Teacher. One who teaches. I realized that what the churches were saying was mostly true, but what they weren't saying was devastating. And what they weren't saying was how does it work. What do we do? They were great at telling us what to think and what to believe and how to pray and how to pay. But what do we do? How do we relieve the pain? There must be more to spirituality than going unconscious once a week to a lot of meaningless words and rituals.

Maybe if they taught people to do those rituals and the meaning of those words it would help. Well, it does help. There is no maybe about it. Actually, it makes all the difference in the world. One priest in San Francisco tried to wake people up in the late 80's and early 90's and was forced into religious silence for one year by the Catholic Church. At the end of that year, he resigned. Sad. Now when I go to one of those churches, I can appreciate what is happening. I understand what they are meaning and what they are doing. Yet, I look around and still see the same blank sleepy faces. It is no wonder that the church's congregations are dwindling while there is a spiritual revolution upon us.

Now days, it is the "New Age" organizations and Teachers that are taking the place of the church and priests. It is sad but true. More and more people are coming to spiritual teachers to receive what they should have received as children in the churches. To be nourished with spiritual truth and understanding. Spirituality was not meant to be a secret or a mystery. It is meant to be understood and practiced by all people in all aspects of life. Today there are few true Teachers in the world, and few true seekers. But somehow, the two come together against all odds and in spite of all manner of obstacles. As is stated in the Bible, "Seek and ye shall find."

Chapter Three

GOD AND CHRIST

In this chapter I will talk about the Christ and Christmas. Mostly about the Christ. But before I begin, I want to briefly talk about God, The Creator, The Supreme Being, The Is, The Universe, The Force, The All, The Essence, The Light, The Source or… however you like to label your own Divinity.

If you could see the face of God, what would you see? In the old days, it was said that it is impossible to see the face of God. Interesting perspective, don't you think? I have wondered why they said that. At the same time, they said that God was an old man with a gray beard. How did they know that? Here's the dichotomy: If they couldn't look into the face of God, how did they know what he looked like? OR: If the old belief that God is an old man with a gray bread was truly what the Masters of old taught, then it should not have been a problem to look into the face of God - but it was. Unless of course that the face of God, although human, was so radiant that it was blinding to the eyes. But, then again, how would we know what he looked like?? And then, we must assume that God could be seen with the human eye to begin with. Too sloppy any way you look at it, if you ask me!

For this reason, I do not think many people in the world today really believe the myth about God being old and gray. But many still believe in the angry, jealous and punishing God. Which makes even less sense than the old man theory! To understand Christ, we must also understand God. And understanding both is essential to our well being as a race of humans living on planet earth.

The true nature of God is very simple, as is all other things in the Universe. God is a collective of all life, intelligent or otherwise, in the Universe. God is the essence, the energy or the light that is in everything created on all levels. It is The Universal Mind, The Love, The Power, The Good and The True. It is me. It is you. It is your boss, your children, and every human being that you have ever met. Every tree, animal, fish, insect, and reptile. God is the rocks, water, air, fire and earth. Every star and planet and all the Angels.

If you were to see God, what would you see? Easy question to answer: You would see a bright and shining vortex of energy. It would be so bright that you would not be able to look directly into it. It would look almost exactly like our physical Sun. White light, awakening all of our consciousness. Warm and almost unbearably Loving. Radiating throughout the Universe from a seemingly central point. The urge is to move closer to the Light, to bathe totally within its love and radiance and to never turn back. This urge is seemingly over powering. Total acceptance and love is what is given to you as you suddenly realize who you are. As you approach this Divine Light, you realize that it is not a solid thing. You see within, that there are levels or layers of Light Beings and that each level inward is a higher and purer consciousness. And that these levels seem endless, and may very well be so.

At some point, you realize that you are one of them. You are one of the countless Light Beings whose consciousness manifests this Universe and the realities that we dwell in. You know that God's Will and your will are one and the same and that you have never been separated from the Creator. It would be an impossibility because your true mind is a piece of God's. God is being you. You are not God, but God is surely you. You are a Son or Daughter of God.

God represents Itself through all beings in the Universe. From the highest of the Angels to all of us humans, God is manifest throughout the Universe and in this world. If we pray to God, we pray to the Cherubs. It is also they who answer the prayers we send. If we need a Miracle, then it is the Dominations that do the work. Each level that we associate with God is manifest through Angel or human.

In the Bible, it is said that Jesus was the only begotten Son of God. Strange. This seems to contradict what I just said about you in the previous paragraphs. What is even stranger, is that Jesus never said that. Actually, Jesus never said many of the things that are said about him in the Bible. If you go through the New Testament and read only the "red letters", only the things that Jesus said, you will get a whole different picture about Jesus and the Christ. Actually, Jesus called himself the "Son of Man". Never did he say the Son of God. What did he mean by that? What did he mean when he said that we will do greater things than him? Or that it is not he who does the work, but the Father who does the work? Why would Jesus make such statements?

See, the problem is that we have been programmed to not really read the Bible… or anything else. We've been programmed to read only what is "allowed" or accepted as valid information. The Christian Churches have worked really hard to make sure that we do not actually understand who Jesus was, who the Christ is and who God is. All they talk about is the "mystery" of the cross, the "mystery" of God, the mystery of the resurrection… Everything is a fucking "mystery" to these people!

Or is it?? Maybe they are withholding vital information for your "protection". Maybe they really know the truth, but have been taught to not give it! Well, the truth is, there is no "maybe" about it. We have been lied to about our divinity. Jesus the Christ was the only one who told the truth and they nailed him to a tree to shut him up about it. Then, over the years, a couple of centuries or so later, the Christians became just like the Jews - except their method was different. Accepting, rather than denying Jesus and the Christ, they decided to make him into an unattainable icon. Almost a myth. Someone that was not like us in any way. Someone who was conceived, came, lived and left differently than we could ever dream of. Someone who was not human, but God incarnated. The opposite of us, according to them. We have "original sin" - Jesus was without sin. God is without sin. Even insects are without sin! But not us. We have sin. But he "died for our sins", didn't he? So how do we have this original sin thing happening? And then, if that was not enough, Christmas – the Christ mass - has been changed into an economic holiday. Everyone only thinking about what they will get from who. The spirit of giving has been squashed by greed and competition to the point where love and true spirituality are not even part of it anymore.

Too many contradictions for my taste. So let's begin to look at reality for a moment. Let's start with the Trinity: The Father, Son and Holy Spirit. Three men, running the whole show… right? That's what they taught me anyway. Well, here begins the problem. First of all, God, being a collective of all intelligent life, cannot be just male or just female. God is both, because God is the all. Simple and hard to argue with. In the Essene Gospel of Peace, (written by the Essenes about the Master Jesus and found in the basement of the Vatican in 1929), the Mother aspect of God is acknowledged throughout by Jesus. He discusses both the Father and Mother aspects repeatedly throughout his lectures to people. (No wonder the Christians hid this from the people!)

The next problem is the Holy Spirit being a male. People do not even know what the Holy Spirit is these days. Do you know why? Because no one has taught about the Holy Spirit. Jesus came and taught us about the Christ mind and showed us who the Christ was. But that has not happened with the Holy Spirit. I suspect that the knowledge is hidden away somewhere in the Vatican. All the people know about is Mary, the mother of Jesus. The pure and loving mother who gives birth to the Son. Even that explains a lot about the nature of the Holy Spirit, if one looks at the spiritual significance.

The Holy Spirit is the Female aspect of God, whose domain is in this dimension. She gives life to this planet, all things. Let's look at it this way: they say God is a man and God created the Universe. How many men do you know that have given birth or created life in a natural way?? Personally, I can't think of any. I can't even think of any that want to! It is not a male principle. The male is needed, yes, but the female is the creative force. BOTH are needed - not just one or the other. "As above, so below", right? What is true here in this world is true here in the spiritual world. The Holy Spirit is the female representitive of what we would call God. She is the power behind the Christ.

The Universe didn't create things that would not make sense or confuse us. Everything fits together, corresponds and makes perfect sense. You just have to be sensible about it. Get rid of the old dogma and avoid the New Age airy-fairy fantasyland syrup, be practical and real, and everything falls into place.

Now let's talk about the Christ. The first thing to realize here is that Jesus and the Christ are two different people. Surprised? Well, it's true. The Christ is the Father aspect of

15

God. Remember: it is the "Father" that does the work. The "Father" was the Christ working through Jesus. Look at the following statements: "Sometimes I am with you and sometimes I am not", "Please Father, take this cup if be your will…" "Father, why have you forsaken me?", "Forgive them Father, for they do not know what they do". These statements demonstrate the duel nature within Jesus. Some are obviously the Christ, an enlightened being, and some are obviously someone whose faith was tested, someone who still needed to grow. If Jesus and the Christ were one in the same, there would have been only the purest expressions coming from the mouth of Jesus. No fear, no doubt and certainly no anger. And, if Jesus was God incarnated, this would be even more perfect.

The truth is that Jesus was a human being - just like we are. And we have the same potentials as he started with. Now, understand that I would not put myself in the same league as Jesus. This was the man who initiated the Christ into our world. And he did it 2000 years ago! We've had 2000 years just to follow his instructions and look what we've done! Not much! In my opinion, he was the greatest Master to ever live on this earth. Still, though, he was human. He had to be, otherwise, the whole Christian religion would be invalid.

Each year, on December 25th, we celebrate the birthday of Jesus. Was that his true birthday? No. Not even close. The reality is that the Christians, who were competing with mostly the pagan religions, stole (borrowed?) that date for their own purpose. Actually it was always a pagan holiday, celebrating the Solstice on the 21st. This is the true Christmas, when each year, on the Solstice, the new and higher vibration of the Christ is given to the planet. So, in a round about way, this can be considered the annual rebirth of the Christ.

16

Evolving
A Spiritual Guide for Living

What is most important is what was taught to us by the Christ through the Master Jesus. The Christ was truly the Way, the Truth and the Life. And when he said, "all that come to the Father must come through me", he was meaning exactly what he said. It does not mean that you must accept Jesus as your Lord and Savior. It does not hurt, but it doesn't guarantee anything either. It means that you must take on for yourself the mind of Christ, as demonstrated by Jesus.

And what did he demonstrate? Good question. One of the first things the Christ says to us in the Bible is "I have good news! Rejoice! You do not need to suffer any longer! The Christ is among you…" How did this turn into original sin and us all being basically evil?! He taught us that we do not have to suffer at all. That we can live in health and happiness. That all things are possible. That God loves us. And all we have to do is love God.

What does that mean? Good question. Who is God?? Go back to paragraph number 4. God is everyone and everything that you see. Even your mother-in-law. (No offense to all mother-in-laws! After all, most of you mothers will be one someday.)

The Christ said to "take my yolk, it is easy". EASY. Did he lie?? Easy!? Why would the Christ say such a thing? If it is so easy, why hasn't the world become Christed? The truth is that the One must now become the Many. We must all become the Christ. This is the destiny of the human race. But easy?! It didn't even look easy for Jesus! Actually, it looked pretty damn hard to me! But what you discover is that as you go, as you practice what was taught, it does become easy. It is just a matter of letting go of the old and moving forward. Isn't that exactly what Christ taught? He told the Rabbis to change their ways, and the people to look at life differently in a new way. And that "your faith has

17

made you whole". That there are many mansions in the Kingdom of God, and treasures beyond belief, and that the Kingdom of God is within, and to not worry about yesterday or tomorrow, that God will provide. Just be here now. The Christ has said the same things through many different masters in this world: Buddha, Krishna, St. Germain, Sai Baba, Mother Theresa, and so many more.

Now, in the New Age, which really is the rebirth of the Christ, or as stated in the Bible, the second coming of Christ, it is time to truly bring to life what was taught. The Christ has been dead in the minds of people for too long. Know that the Christ ensouled this planet when Jesus' blood dripped into the earth while he hung on the cross. Know that communion is not on Sunday morning in church, but every time you eat, drink or breath, because all of this dimension is about the marriage between the Holy Spirit and the Christ. Realize that every cell in your body is made of the Christ mind. And know that you are a vital part of the Sonship and you are needed now to bring Light into the world. Think of the Christ always, not just on December 25th. And when you do, think of the Christ as you - the second coming. The One must become the Many and it begins now with you.

Below is a gift for you written by Marianne Williamson:

Our Deepest Fear

Our deepest fear is *not* that we are inadequate.

Our deepest fear is that we are powerful beyond measure.

It is our Light, not our darkness that most frightens us.

We ask ourselves, who am I to be brilliant, gorgeous, talented, fabulous?

Actually, who are you NOT to be?

You are a Child of God. Your playing small does not serve the world.

There is nothing enlightened about shrinking so that other people won't feel insecure around you.

We were born to make manifest the glory of God that is within us.

It is not just in some of us; it is in everyone.

And as we let our own Light Shine, we unconsciously give other people permission to do the same.

As we are liberated from our own fear, our presence automatically liberates others.

Chapter Four

THE MIRACLE OF BIRTH

I have witnessed eleven physical births. Every one of them was simply amazing. I cannot think of anything in the world that has moved me as much as seeing a soul being born into their physical body. It is always an honor to be present at the birth of a being, whether you are the father or not.

The first birth I saw was the birth of my oldest son. After 13 hours of writing down contractions on little slips of paper, and then flying to the hospital at incredibly fast speeds, the blessed event happened. In those days, I knew little about childbirth, even though I went through all of the parental training programs. Like most people, we went to classes to find out how to do what people have been doing naturally forever, and then, eventually just to realize that the birth will happen regardless of how many hours of training is taken. During the labor, things went well for a while, until a certain point, then suddenly, for no apparent reason, my sweet, kind and gentle wife turned on me like I was the devil incarnate. Every time I said anything, like "It's OK honey, you're doing fine", she would reply with "Go to hell you fucking bastard!". To say the least, I was shocked. Of course, when she bit almost entirely through my hand during a contraction, I began to question my role in the whole birthing process.

Needless to say, the baby came - they always do. My son, my first born, the thing that we so enthusiastically created and waited for, emerged from my wife's body. From where I was standing, I couldn't actually see him coming out. Good thing. I say this because when I did see him, I wanted to run out of the room! At first, I thought we had created an alien lizard! He was not only the ugliest thing I had ever seen, but he kept changing colors! He did improve though. After about 5 minutes, he looked like Henry Kissinger, but uglier, if that is possible. But that is not the most shocking thing that happened.

The most shocking thing was my wife's reaction, which I prepared for. I wanted to prepare her before she actually saw him, but I couldn't speak, so I just stepped away, thinking she would probably attack me for creating a lizard that looked like Kissinger. After all, my hand was still bleeding and my ego was still bruised. But, to my surprise, upon looking at this… thing, she smiled, took him in her arms and said how beautiful he was! BEAUTIFUL! "Strange", I thought to myself. Later on that night, my mother came in and looked at the baby and said "How darling".

Now, I could understand my wife's reaction in a weird and abstract way, after all, she *had* to love it. There is an uncontrollable force of nature that over powers the senses of a new mother, and even though I didn't quite understand this at that moment, I was sensing it had to be something like that. But my mother? Well my mother had ulterior motives. She had experience with 5 of her own children. She knew what I didn't know.

Let's back up in time a little. When I was in the University in the mid 1970's, I studied Biology, Physiology, Psychology and Genetics. Something I realized then was that the most natural way to have a baby was in a squatting position. This I realized would help to open up the whole pelvic area. But, I thought, who am I to talk about these things? I figured that if they have women lying on their backs, with their feet up in stirrups, pushing a baby out of their body going uphill, against gravity and everything else, then there must be a good reason for it. Well, there is: it is easier for the doctor.

So now we begin. This was the first of many realizations about the birthing process. I will talk here about both the incredible miracles of birth on all levels and the things that have been created to destroy the miracles of birth, also on all levels.

Society, for centuries, have methodically taken away the power and authority of women. Birthing is probably the most critical. Giving birth to a living being is one of the most important initiations that a woman will take. The whole experience surpasses everything else possible on this planet. How can I, a mere male, know this? I have been told, not only by the Masters, but also by very powerful women. Plus I have been a witness to this and many other connected events.

Unfortunately, women today have been programmed by doctors, priests, mothers, and other women that having a baby is torture, punishment, demeaning, dis-empowering, foolish and is not an experience that one has power or authority over. Doctors have created a system that requires total dependency. Pregnant women are treated like they have a disease or disability. Religions talk about the suffering that women must bare because of the seduction or Adam some thousands of years ago. Mothers proudly tell their baby girls how much unbearable pain they will experience someday. And feminists talk about how only stupid cows would have babies and become full time mothers.

Where is the positive input? Where is the talk about the miracle of birth, the power that comes with creation, the joy and fulfillment, the growth and prosperity that children can bring? Well, in these things, for most people, there is no pride or profit. No way to control or torment. No way to build themselves up or to feel important. So the truth about birth is ignored. And girls become women who view birth with negativity or even terror.

How does this affect the child? It is known that the baby, while in the womb, feels whatever the mother is feeling. It is also known that the baby can hear the mother's voice as well as other voices speaking to the mother. Many times, it has been noted how a baby will respond to the father's voice just after birth. Spiritually speaking, the baby knows the mother and the father intimately. The spirit is present consciously with the parents from before conception and of course all through the pregnancy. As soon as the egg is fertilized, there is a conscious living being growing a physical body. It is aware of everything that is happening and that is said during that time. So it feels the mother's fears and apprehensions about the birthing process.

This is not highly detrimental for the infant, but it does have an effect, especially upon the birth. For example, in most countries, Caesarean Section (C-Section) has become extremely common. Many C-Sections are done at the first sign of risk or even difficulty. The vast majority of C-Sections are not even necessary, but are done for the convenience of the Doctor or because of fear from the mother.

This is unfortunate for the baby. Many people think it is a good thing for the baby to have an easy birth, but the reality is that in most cases, the baby needs to go through the birth canal. Spiritually, emotionally and physically, the baby needs to be squeezed as it begins life on this planet. It is not traumatic! It is the very first initiation, the first active and conscious step forward that a spirit takes. It gives the new born a chance to participate in its own birth and gives the first lesson in follow through, completion, achievement, determination and commitment. If you have had a child, then you know that that is what was required for you to deliver the baby. So the baby learns this from the mother and from its own required participation. (Remember, we are talking about conscious beings here! Just because they cannot speak like us when they are born does not mean that they do not know what is going on!) Consequently, many C-Section children have trouble throughout life completing projects, work or assignments.

Maybe 30% of the time a C-Section is necessary. In those cases, other lessons are involved. But when a doctor or programmed fear creates this path, then both the mother and the child are robbed of the initiation, and the learning opportunity. This path of birth is repeated many times in life with many other learning lessons and initiations. The child probably will have another chance to receive this initiation, but not the experience and most times the mother will not have another opportunity. In most cases, doctors have convinced women that if you have one C-section, then all of your children must be born that way. Of course, this is just another lie.

How to correct this aspect of birthing is difficult. The doctors have so much authority over women today that it is virtually unheard of for a woman to stand up to a doctor and tell him or her what she wants. And if she does, then the doctor will play the fear/guilt card, telling the mother that she is endangering the life of the baby. In most cases this is not true, but the mother has no choice but to believe the doctors and do whatever they say. This is because most people have not really done the work to learn the realities of birthing. They just sit and listen to whatever is told to them, and act accordingly without question. And questioning is the key.

Evolving
A Spiritual Guide for Living

If you become pregnant, you have nine months to learn about this thing that is going to happen. Do the research! Find the truth! And then, if you use a doctor, question the doctor's actions, motives and perspectives! Force them to prove to you that they are truly making the correct decisions! Realize that it is not the decision of the doctor, it is your decision and no one else's! Who says you cannot question "established" authority? Because people are afraid to question, women today deliver their children in ridiculous positions, under insane circumstances, being guided by self important, ego maniacs that are more interested in profit and convenience than in the true well being of the humans involved.

Then comes the fear issue. Fear of pain or death is a compelling illusion. These days, few women, if any, die giving birth. So that one can easily be let go of. Just check the statistics, it is so rare that it is barely even a number. Fear of pain on the other hand is a different story. I have yet to hear a woman say that the delivery of her child was painless. Although, I have read about cultures where the women deliver without pain. What I actually know about pain is this: All pain is emotional, mental or expected. It is then translated to the body. If it is eliminated from the mind and the emotions, then it will not exist in the body. But I must tell you that the expectation of pain that has been programmed into the mind from childhood by generations of prideful and malicious mothers, is difficult to eliminate. But not impossible. I have seen women work on themselves during pregnancy and create relatively easy births. In this case, work is the key. You must deprogram and reprogram the subconscious and conscious minds for a normal, natural humane birth. Humane for you and for the baby.

What happens next, when the baby if finally born in the hospital is outrageous. The mother sees the baby for a

25

matter of minutes, then the child is taken away from the mother to be cleaned, checked and tested. First of all, the baby should never leave the mother for at least 72 hours. This is an important transition period for the baby into a new dimension. Instead of being secured and comforted at the bosom of the mother, it is put under glaring bright lights; it's sensitive skin is scrubbed, causing pain and removing all of the important nutrients and substances created to protect the skin for that 72 hours; and then if that is not enough, they use needles to inject chemicals and to take blood! What a way to begin life! Instant trauma! And for what? They bleed babies to test for diseases that are one in 4,000,000 at the most. The things that they are injecting into the body is already in the mother's milk. Actually, everything the baby needs is in the mother and in her milk. So immediately the soul is not only traumatized, but kicked out of the body.

If the mother had a C-Section, it can even be worse. Many times the mother is knocked out by the drugs and cannot breast-feed the baby for several hours. This causes extreme pain for the mother and it creates an instant lack for the baby. Often the baby will get jaundice, or the blood sugar levels will drop. When this happens, the doctors will further traumatize the baby. For jaundice, they will tape the baby's eyes shut and put him/her under bright lights. For blood sugar they will put in an IV and tie him/her down so that he/she doesn't move around. All that is needed to heal jaundice is to put the baby in a window with sunlight coming through. Within a day or two the baby's skin will be back to normal. Mother's milk will heal the blood sugar problem immediately.

One last thing: it has been medically proven that the safest place to have a baby is at home. Statistically, there are fewer problems during and after birth when at home.

Partially because the baby is already immune to everything in the house-just as you are. Also because the environment is more friendly, everyone is more relaxed and more comfortable, especially the mother. This makes the whole process more gentle and nurturing. Now days, there are many midwives that deliver babies at home in most countries. These births are non-traumatic for the both the mother and especially for the baby. Birth trauma is caused by the unnatural medical birthing processes that has been forced down the throats of humanity. My question is, who let the doctors get involved in birthing anyway?!

On the positive side, when the baby takes that first breath, wherever that is, the soul takes full possession of the body. At that moment, the whole room explodes with energy. The room turns to gold on an energy level and the Angels rejoice in song and the true power of the being is manifested in the body.

If you look into the eyes of a newborn baby, the clarity is astounding. Even though they are not supposed to see, they look directly into your eyes. For a short period of time, they are fully conscious beings looking through a pure vehicle. To consciously witness this is something that is indescribable. The best of the mother and the father has been created into a new life form. The child represents the highest essence of the parent's divine love for one another. This energy that has created the baby transcends the conscious awareness to a place of purity and love. Thus, all souls are created in a state within the spiritual realms of love and purity.

After birth, the spirit drifts in and out of the body for five or six months. When the soft spot on the top of the head closes (seventh chakra), then the spirit is sealed into the body. Then, life is a continual rebirth after rebirth. Each time a soul advances to a new level, or takes an initiation,

Michael C. Fikaris

the birthing process is repeated - in the positive way. Little by little, we move closer to the rebirth of our true selves, the "higher self".

Because of the needed learning lessons, and the condition of society today, most people in the world have forgotten who they are. People have taken on programming and characteristics of others, neglecting to really look inside to discover their own true nature or their own true being. So rather than being themselves, they are mostly being something else. This manifests in the life as problems, conflicts, negative emotions, diseases, poverty and so on. Each time a person moves through these things, and eliminates who they are not, then they are reborn to a new level or really, a new life.

Going through this process of evolution and rebirth is similar to being born into the body. One develops spiritually, or in consciousness and awareness, then the person must move from one reality to another. Doing that is often difficult. It takes follow through, completion, determination and commitment. The same things that are necessary for physical birthing. The initiate must let go of the old familiar and comfortable life and venture into the unknown - a whole new reality. Each time this happens we come closer to our true rebirth. A time when we once again take full conscious possession of the physical body. A time when we are clothed in purity and love.

During these processes, we give birth to something pure and genuine. And although we have to go through hell to get there, it is this hell that shows us what we need to do to purify ourselves and the life we have created.

Why did we take on all of this to begin with? Learning. Shortly after physical birth, we begin to take all of the negatives that we need to learn our lessons here on earth. Then at some point, after living with this stuff for many years, we begin to transmute it. Doing this teaches us what it was we needed to learn here. As this happens, from out of the hell and garbage within, is born the most incredible gifts, such as: spiritual truths and understanding; new abilities; happiness and joy; love; and prosperity on all levels. In essence, other forms of birth.

THE SOLSTICE

At the Winter Solstice, something very special happens. A different kind of birth. Traditionally, in the Christian community, Christmas is celebrated as the birth of Jesus. This date of course is not the birth date of Jesus, and I believe that even the Catholics know that. But nonetheless, this is a very important time of the year.

The year can be divided into seven parts or cycles. The first cycle begins on the Winter Solstice, which falls usually on the 21st of December and sometimes on the 22nd. The last cycle of the planet begins on October 31st. (It is interesting that most countries have holidays on these dates.) During this cycle before the Solstice, the planet is in what we call it's "Death Cycle". This is a time of letting go. A time to bring "death" to the old things in your life that are not working for you and to prepare for the birth of the new. During this time, we should especially eliminate the negative things like addictions or destructive relationships or situations, throw away or give away old things, etc.

Then we are reborn again on the Solstice, (now days, we celebrate this on the 25th). This rebirth is symbolized by the giving of new gifts. We have eliminated the old and we are bringing in the new. In reality, the first day of the year, on a planetary level, is also on the Solstice - this being the first day of the first planetary cycle.

29

Michael C. Fikaris

Simultaneously, during the Winter Solstice, we are also given a new level of Christ force energy. Hence the name "Christmas". This energy is given by the Universe at a higher level, a level which the people can handle for the coming year. For three months it multiplies and regenerates in the center of the planet, between the Solstice and the Spring Equinox and it is then released. This was demonstrated to us by Jesus who regenerated in the tomb (inside the earth) for three days (three months) and then resurrected (coming of spring).

On the Winter Solstice day, there is a great celebration in the spiritual world and the doors to the heavens are open. Angels from all of the hierarchies are allowed to freely come into this dimension for one day and we humans can more easily connect and communicate with them. And all who are aware rejoice in the Creator's greatest gift to humanity: The regeneration of life, for this is the energy that brings us the spring, the summer and the fall. This is the energy that, when married with the Holy Spirit, (the female aspect of God), grows our food, nourishes our bodies, heals and raises our consciousness.

Two Thousand years ago, the Christ ensouled the planet. In other words, the Christ is the soul of this planet. So, when the Christ said through Jesus "When you eat, think of me, and when you drink, think of me...", He was meaning that He has become all things of this earth. He is the gift of Life: "I am the way and truth and the Life". Whenever you eat anything, you are eating the Christ energy, whenever you drink anything, you are drinking the Christ energy, whenever you breathe, you are breathing in the Christ. There is no way around it. And it doesn't matter what name you put upon it. It just is. And the Christ is reborn each and every year at a new level, at a higher vibration according to our needs. So each year, as you

30

celebrate what we call Christmas, remember that the Creator never stops giving the best of all gifts: Life.

Chapter Five

ENERGY

Everything is energy. Everything that you have in your life, whether it is physical, mental, emotional or spiritual, is energy based. The essence of all things is energy. Even your relationships with people are based upon energy: an exchange of energy between two people is what a relationship really is. It is said that God is the all of everything. This is true because God is the Light, and the Light is Energy and everything has this substance or Energy or Light or God within it. Everything we create in this realm begins in the mind as an energy from thought or intent, either from the conscious or unconscious mind.

Each of us has created our own lives through agreement with others and through the use of our energy. The Law of Cause and Effect states that "every cause has its effect; every effect has its cause; everything happens according to law; chance is but a name for law not recognized; there are many planes of causation, but nothing escapes the law". Everything in our lives, physical, emotional, mental, spiritual and good, bad or ugly can be traced to our own actions, words, thoughts, and/or perspectives. This of course requires that the person is brutally honest with themselves and understands that the only path to true power comes from being blameless and completely responsible for his or her own life.

Where your attention goes, your energy flows. Just sit down and put your attention on any one of your fingers for a few minutes. With your eyes, look at that finger and you will notice the energy increasing in your finger. You will

32

actually feel the energy increasing there. This is not something that I just thought of today. This is something that has been scientifically proven. Just by looking at something or someone, energy flows from the area of your eyes and forehead, to that object. Scientists have captured this fact on film. The film shows that where the person is looking there is a flow of energy to the object. But why is there energy from this area to the object? When we physically look at something, we are receiving images, not sending anything from the eyes. It is putting attention on an object that creates the energy pattern that the scientists have seen. That energy does not come from the eyes, but from the mind and through the eyes.

Where your attention goes, your energy flows. The same thing is happening as you think of things. The more you think of something the more of your energy is going to that thing. It is just like "looking" at it on another level. Now sit down again and this time close your eyes and think of, or put your attention on one of your fingers. You will notice the same thing happening as before with your eyes open. Maybe even more so. If you actually do this exercise, you will realize that the energy does not come from the eyes, but from somewhere else. Many of you will be able to "see" your finger in your mind's eye as you do this. If you have this experience, realize who is seeing the finger. The mind cannot operate on it's own or actually see anything. It is you the spirit that sees and controls the mind; and therefore, it is you the spirit that puts attention. So this energy that flows from you to others or other objects comes from your attention as a spirit.

Where your attention goes, your energy flows. How does this fact of life affect us in a practical way each and every day? On a positive level, this knowledge can be a powerful tool. Those who have learned to eliminate

33

Michael C. Fikaris

negative thinking can create in the positive just by focusing upon what they want to create in life. Focusing your attention on your desires is one of the basic principles of manifesting. As you focus, so do you create. Everything begins as energy, comes through you by attention as thought and intent and is manifested in your reality. As you focus your attention upon the desired object, the energy created attracts the object to you or creates the experience in your life.

Where your attention goes, your energy flows. Whatever you are putting your attention on each day is what you are creating or maintaining in your life. Your energy will support or feed your reality according to your thoughts, fears, intent and actions. What mostly blocks us from creating healthy, wealthy, happy and whole lives on all levels is the past. In reality, everything you see is in past time. You only see the past in all things unless they are totally new to you. In other words, your reality today is totally based upon the past. Your past experiences have carved and shaped your perspective of reality. For example, how a Scandinavian person would perceive a cold and snowy winter is much different than how a native Hawaiian would view such an experience. Both perspectives are based upon past experience. One has anchored childhood memories of joyfully playing in the snow. The other has never experienced life below 18 Celsius and may have great fear of such brutal cold that he has never come close to experiencing before. Likewise, the person who spent their entire life in poverty could not perceive himself as obtaining wealth; while the person born in wealth cannot perceive himself as being poor. Consequently, in most cases, these people will continue creating the same circumstances throughout life. So we look upon life as we have experienced it. And how we experience life is very subjective according to how you have been taught or programmed. Your experience dictates your perspective.

We were taught to believe that 1+1=2. Everyone in the world, it seems, agrees with this. But, strictly speaking, according to the science of nuclear physics, 1+1=2.3 because the action of adding the numbers adds more to the original essence. So much of our lives are based upon past information, even the most basic things that we believe in or operate daily upon.

Most people never question the old accepted perspectives in their lives, only the new ideas. And then, that examination of new things is based upon old concepts that have been blindly accepted. The problem with that is that most of people's old perspectives were programmed in at an age before questioning. If a parent tells the child that the grass is green and the snow is white, why would the child question it? If the parent tells the child that there is no money or opportunity for money, why would the child question? There is no basis for the child to question. Only total trust in the parent. Then, many years down the road, the parent's beliefs have become the child's, without question. The past becomes the present from generation to generation.

Where your attention goes, your energy flows. Have you ever noticed how people keep recreating the same problems, the same situations, the same relationships over and over again? You would think that they would learn the lesson and move on. But nooooo, they keep reliving the same things over and over and over and over again. What is the problem here?! Well, it should be quite obvious by now. These people are continually bringing their past into their present and their future.

One of the bad habits that has been passed down to each generation is hanging on to things in a negative way. People have been programmed with so much fear of losing things in life that they have developed the habit of not being able to let go. Unfortunately, out of fear of the unknown, people hang onto the very things in life that are literally killing them: resentment, prejudice, fear, hate, anger, envy, greed, gluttony, slothfulness, lust, competition, self importance, pride and victimism.

The only way out is in. The only way in, is to let go. Let go of the past first, then let go of everything else. "To have all, you must first give all". The only way to truly have anything is to first let it go. There is a saying that says, "If you truly love someone, set them free. If he or she returns, then you have found true love." This applies to everything in life. Whatever we try to possess or hold on to we will lose, whatever we resist we will get. What belongs to you for your use on this planet will be with you, the rest is just extra baggage that will drag you down and wear you out.

Learning to truly let go allows you to flow through life rather than constantly struggling. Too often people try to force life to happen the way they want it. Or if it doesn't happen the way they want it, then they are upset or angry or sad or even depressed. What people do not realize is that life is happening the way they are creating it. But by not letting go, the universe is teaching them hard lessons.

It is like when I told my son when he was four years old not to piss on the house plants anymore and he did it again anyway. He had to be punished so that he would learn the simple lesson of not pissing on mommy's house plants. From his perspective, I was being mean because I wouldn't let him do what he wanted to do, and if it was OK to piss outside on a bush, he should be able to piss inside on a bush too. Then he wanted to debate why he got in trouble for pissing in the kitchen sink. Since it was going down the drain anyway, what's the difference? Pretty soon, I was spending most of my quality time with my four-year-old son discussing the ethics of pissing. It took him a long time to let go of this pissing thing and it cost him many days busted in his room. This is exactly what people do in their lives on a daily basis. They demand that they want to do something and the universe says "No". But they do it again anyway or they mope about it forever rather than just letting go and moving on to bigger and better things.

Do you know how to make God laugh? Tell Him your plans. It is good to have a plan, but you don't have to be married to it. Often, it is appropriate to make a change, to walk away. Too many people in the world today are hanging on to dead marriages, jobs, belief systems, perspectives, relationships, healing programs and spiritual concepts. Rather than fighting for meaningless leftovers, why not let go and let the Universe give you a banquet of life's experiences. Are you still resenting people and experiences from the past? Let them go! Get off of it for Christ's sake! You are just feeding death!

For most people in this world, it is too difficult to let go. For many, a familiar stuck and "dependable" hell is preferred over the unknown flow of heaven. The personality hates change and unfortunately, the personality controls the conscious life of almost all people. To make a profound change in one's life, the individual soul must take control back from the personality and then let it go to the Creator.

To put yourself into the flow of life, all you must do is to let go and let God. Each day, turn your life over to the Creator. Stop trying to control, to manipulate, to hold on to or possess. When something doesn't go the way you planned, just step back, let it go and realize that what is happening is part of the divine plan for your life. Daily, turn your life over to the universe to guide you. Pray that the Creator's Will be done in all things and then bring your attention into the present, let go and step into the flow of life, of love and of heaven on earth!

Chapter Six

THE GAME OF LIFE

Things are really changing in the world! There is no doubt about that. Just take a look at your own life. If you are paying attention, you will realize that changes are happening at this very moment. The only thing that is constant, is change. Everything is in a constant state of change. The problem is that people try to resist change and in some cases are very successful at changing very little. The essence of Life itself is about change. This whole dimension was created by an outburst of spontaneous life-force energy. That burst of energy changed everything in the Universe, physically and spiritually. By trying to control that energy by holding it back within yourself, and thereby blocking change within yourself, you are merely blocking your vital life-force energy. Living naturally in this universe means to let go and allow yourself to go with the flow of life. Life is not about structure, it is about fluidity. Structure, rules, and constraints have been put upon all humans in order to keep us under the control of the few. These "few" fear change, therefore they have defined what they would like the game of life to be: a game that is easily managed by them, yet not fulfilling for us.

The true game of Life is an easy game to play. You just need to know the rules of the game. There are many games going on here. There are as many games as there are people. One of the most popular games on this planet is the "Sleep" game or the "I am not really aware of what I am doing" game. These people do not even know that what they are doing is playing a game. They believe (or pretend to believe) that they are just being themselves most or even all of the time. If questioned directly, most people will eventually admit that they are acting most of the time. But a certain amount of willingness to be truthful is required in order to admit such a thing.

The problem with games is that once a person finds a game that he likes, he doesn't want to change it. That stops true growth. Many believe that they are growing when really they are not, they are just adjusting the game or making slight variations of the game which gives the appearance of growth. And then they try to convince themselves and others that they are on the spiritual path. Usually, they are successful at fooling themselves and others because there is no real awareness of what is real and what is false. Game players are always suckers for games. Most people judge others by how they are treated by those people. For example, if someone is nice to you and strokes your ego, then you may decide that this person is a good and spiritual person. Or someone who once treated you badly and now suddenly treats you nicely may be someone you see as growing spiritually. What a joke! Why not see through the game? Why not realize that the person probably just wants something from you and she knows that stroking your ego is the fastest way to get it? Well, that then would be painful for the ego. And the ego controls the game...

The personality loves to play the "comfort" game. The personality hates change of any kind, it is literally threatened by change because it cannot control change. No one can, really. Therefore, the personality has created a comfort zone, where everything is under its control. No threats or challenges exist here, unless threats and challenges are what it is accustomed to. In such a case, the lack of threats and challenges would be threatening to the personality. The comfort zone has no direction whatsoever, it's only purpose is to maintain the status quo. This path is so wide that people can get the illusion of moving forward, of progress, of growth, or whatever they are looking for - anything to make them feel comfortable and valid at the same time.

One comfort zone is the spiritual concept of "one size fits all". People take it on as a part of themselves. It's like asking "why", and the answer is an explanation of an explanation. This is the acceptance of standard answers to questions that are really not answerable. These are things that can be only experienced, not intellectualized. Or, accepting religious dogma, whether new age or old age, (makes no difference), both are designed to hold the person in a certain state of consciousness – within a structure. In this case, spiritual concepts are vaguely given without substance or the possibility of substance. For example: "the mystery of the cross"; the resurrection; the "face of God"; dying unto self; the Light; and Divine Love. To understand these spiritual realities, one must run out of the comfort zone of spirituality and venture into the "unknown" reality of spirituality. But that may be "uncomfortable". After all, look what the great masters had to go through to obtain these things. Jesus, being our best example: 40 days in the desert, beaten, tortured, betrayed, and crucified. Who is inspired to do these things? Who even WANTS to be inspired to do these things?? The comfort zone game works quite well for obvious reasons.

I learned at a young age that the easiest person to sell something to is a salesperson. Once I realized this, I asked myself "Why is this true?" Later in life I realized that people play games that they are not aware of. Actually, they believe that their games are real, that is why they are not aware of playing the game. Therefore, if someone plays the same game on them, then they believe that person is

41

expressing reality, or being real, and then they respond accordingly.

As a teenager, while dating and learning about women, I had an idea once. Noticing that the young girls I was dating were prone to emotional outbursts of crying, whenever given a chance, I thought I would try the same game on them. I would bring up an emotion strong enough for me to manufacture tears in front of the girl I wanted to affect. Well, needless to say, it worked wonders. Later I discovered that victims were always suckers for victims, egomaniacs were always attracted to egomaniacs... and so on. Everyone falls subject to their own game.

Take a look at the Middle East for a moment. Here we have literally millions of people caught up in a game that started a very long time ago by people that are now long dead. But this game is so fixed into their minds as reality, that they cannot see any way out of the game, and in fact, they use most of their energy feeding and supporting the game – all in the name of God! This is an accepted way of life for them. For most of us, we can look at this ridiculous situation, and wonder "how in the world can this be continuing on in this day and age?" But it does.

Most games are far more subtle, yet just as destructive. Maybe, even more so. At least in the Middle East, the people know that there is a problem. The rest of the world is sleeping, believing that everything is fine, ok, wonderful, and even great. All the while, being someone else, doing things unconsciously, emotionally defective and never manifesting the life you were born to have.

The games are numerous. Too numerous to mention in this little chapter of this little book. But I will mention a few of the big ones. Let's start with the most popular type of game: the White game. The white game is the game where the person appears to be good, but really there is something missing. I know this game well, because I played it for so long. As I was growing up, I was always the talented one, the good son, and eventually the successful one. I supported my family, (mother, stepfather, two sisters and brother), for many years. I had the wife, two children, nice house, a couple of cars, some businesses, and plenty of money to share with everyone – which I did. I was never convicted of any crimes. I didn't cheat on my wife. And my business practices were honest and fair at all times. Seemingly, I was truly a good person. The problem was that one-day I woke up. And when I woke up, I saw really what I was doing. I saw that under this All-American nice guy image, was something completely different. And that I was using all of them to fulfill my own needs, wants and desires. And my own illusions of grandeur. To accomplish this, I used their weakness for money. I gave them enough to keep them faithful, and enough to keep them from having to care for themselves, which made them dependent upon me. That made me feel secure and important. It fed my ego and my pride. And in return, they were fed and housed like a bunch of worthless sheep being prepared for slaughter.

White games come in many forms: the loving, yet interfering parent; the priest who does not empower the congregation; the politician who works to control the masses for his own profit; the school teacher that programs the child to be like everyone else; the loving wife that cries for more and more attention; the providing husband that is too caught up in his own little kingdom to pay attention to anyone else's needs; the great healers that can only talk about themselves; the spiritual teacher that says one thing and demonstrates another; the Millionaire that gives fortunes to charities and cannot give an ounce of love to his children; the friend in need who hates you for needing him; etc. White games. Subtle, yet dangerous. Usually, more dangerous for the person playing the game than for anyone else. But not always. This game creates a false appearance of goodness or of light.

This brings me to the most dangerous of all white games: false spirituality. This is also probably the oldest white game on the planet: people pretending to be holy and true. Pretending to have a special place in the world. Or pretending to have an exclusive access to God. These are people that believe that they are truly better than those that they are supposed to serve. These are people that believe they are special or the chosen ones, sent here as God's gift to humanity. These are the ones that couldn't save their own souls if their lives depended upon it, and it does, and they don't. They mix the truth with lies and illusions, offering vague promises of heaven, all the while making sure people feel guilty and unworthy of even a glance of heaven. These are the priests, ministers, gurus, healers and new age teachers. These people are male and female alike, young and old and of every race and color. This game is so instilled within all nations that it is almost impossible for most to see it. Now days, the more "awake" people are trading the old white game for a newer one called "New Age". It is still the same old game though, just played at a "higher level". People think that if they meditate once in a while, burn incense and candles, play new age music and talk about past lives that they are spiritual. People believe that just because someone has written a book and claims to talk to angels that that person is for real. It is a variation on the same old game. The appearance is of growth, but movement does not necessarily mean growth. Movement must go forward to be considered growth.

And the ultimate white game: the game of "No Game". This one is becoming more popular these days. The "no game" game gives the person a sense of freedom. They feel that they can do anything that seems real to them. They can speak "honestly" and openly to others. "Honestly" meaning that they can say whatever they really want to say, whether it is really honest or not. They feel that they can do whatever they want, otherwise, it would be playing a game not to.

The problem with this game is that the reality is that everyone is playing one game or another. You have to be in a game to be here on this planet. This whole planet is an illusion, therefore, to be here, you are at least playing the game of human life on earth, rather than life in the real world.

Then we have the Black games. The black games are easy to see: killers; rapists; child abusers; thieves; embezzlers; adulterers; weapons dealers; drug dealers; alcohol dealers; cigarette dealers; butchers; etc. This type of game is obviously destructive or evil in nature.

Next we have a few games that are not White games and are not Black games either. They somehow fall into a gray zone. For example, competition between people. It is obviously not a white game, and we can't clearly put it into the black game section either. Yet, it is not a valid game to play.

Another example is survival games. People will do anything based upon money these days. They make all of their decisions based upon what they think something is worth monetarily, or how much they think they can afford. Business transactions are not always what they should be, but they are acceptable according to society. Again, difficult to classify. It is not pretending to be good, and it is not obviously evil. Yet it is a destructive consciousness and a destructive game nonetheless.

Lastly, we have the Gold game. The Gold game requires integrity on all levels. This is not acquired overnight, but must be worked upon consistently over time. Having integrity means being spiritually integrated within the body and mind. What this means is that you as a spirit must come into this dimension through your body and mind and express your true nature at all times. When this truly happens, there is no conflict or disharmony on any level. Your perspective, thoughts, words and actions all match according to who you are. And all four of these aspects of you are in harmony with one another. In other words, you do not think one thing and say another, and then do something else completely different. Your actions, words, thoughts and perspective continually demonstrate who you are and what your intentions in this dimension are. There is no split, division, conflict or separation on any level. When people look at you, they get what they see. No more, no less. You are an open book, immune from the games of distraction, hiding and illusion. When the game is played from this level, people will see and love you for who you are rather than who you want them to see. Being loved for who you are makes life so simple because you don't have to keep up the illusion that you have created. The important thing about this game is to be real and consistent at all times. That is what makes it easier as time goes on.

The gold game is the only game in town worth playing. This game is a win-win game all of the time. Here we find the true servers of humanity. The true healers, teachers, leaders, supporters,... well, let's just say the true human beings. Real people. The gold game is easy to play once you truly understand games. All you need to do is to become totally unselfish and non-self centered; to truly want to serve the Universe; to see the Light in all people and in all situations; and then to think, speak and act accordingly, or how you would expect the Christ, the Holy Spirit, Jesus, Buddha, Krishna, St. Germain or any other master to think, speak and act. No excuses, no rationales, and no "good reasons" why you can't. (These too are just more games! And "can't" should not exist in your vocabulary!) These people played the Gold game - the game of Life. Thereby, living in reality. "What is real cannot be threatened, what is not real does not exist".

Look at your life. What is real? What is not? Whatever is not real, no longer give it attention, no longer feed it and no longer act according to that illusion or game. Take what is real, truly real, and begin to build upon that. These are the rules of the game of Life. In the Gold game, everybody wins. In reality, it is the only game in town!

Chapter Seven

FREEDOM

Freedom is something that people throughout history have fought and died for. Even today, there are freedom fighters throughout the world, sacrificing their physical bodies for this thing called freedom. The price of freedom cannot be measured, negotiated or bartered. The price must be paid by the beneficiary… in full.

I have found that this is something that most people in all parts of the world seem to understand on one level or another. Those with the deepest understanding are those who have realized their own loss of freedom. This realization is shocking at first to most people because it is within our most basic nature to be free. But because of this, most people refuse to see the true condition of their life in regards to personal freedom. On the surface, most people believe that they are free. This is necessary to rationalize their existence or present living conditions. But then upon further scrutiny, most will realize that in reality, they have very little or no freedom whatsoever. For these people, there are very few moments of joy, pleasure or fulfillment. Life is like a prison in which most are trapped into daily routines, forever repeating the dull, daily drudgery that is so absurdly called "life". Trapped because there seemingly is no way out. Once you are in, it is very difficult to escape and eventually, the thought of escape does not even occur. All the focus of energy is directed to just surviving, or doing the time. The problem for most is that by the time the sentence is completed, the person is too worn out to really enjoy, experience pleasure or know fulfillment. Not worn out from age, but worn out from so many decades of living in survival, struggling from week to week… doing time.

Years ago I owned a convenience store in Emeryville, CA., and my Teacher would come every night and sit behind the counter on a stool and teach while I waited on customers for about eight hours. One night, while I was stacking cartons of Marlboro cigarettes and my Teacher was talking, something amazing happened to me. I suddenly snapped on a mental level. I realized that I was a spirit. I mean really realized - beyond any shadow of doubt. There was no more wondering, hoping or speculation. The feeling from this knowledge was exhilarating beyond description. I instantly, (sitting there with the cartons of Marlboros in my hands), reached a state of complete joy and freedom. For me, having this realization of self as spirit was the ultimate experience.

Now let me give you little history so that you can understand my reaction: From the time I was 15 years old, my life was dedicated to freedom. Everything I was doing was for one sole (soul) purpose: to set myself free and later to enable my family to be free. I worked toward this constantly all of the time. I took extreme measures to obtain personal freedom because I could not imagine anything more important than this. The funny thing is that I really didn't understand the urgency I had towards freedom. I thought that the masses were controlled by financial means. And that freedom meant to have enough money so that no one else could control me because of my lack of money. To me, money was power and power brought freedom.

What I didn't realize is that freedom was not what I thought. I was striving for financial freedom. I didn't know that there was an inner freedom that could be obtained, regardless of the financial condition of the person. In fact, the only freedom comes from within. Once I understood that freedom could not be bought, I was very happy, for it was that truth that had finally set me free.

So needless to say, when I snapped intellectually I was thrilled. From that point on, my life changed profoundly and permanently. From that time on, everywhere I went, I looked at people differently. I knew that we were all spirits in bodies and suddenly everyone looked different to me. In fact, everything in the world looked different to me. I would go downtown to the bank and just sit in my car on the corner and look at people sometimes for hours. Seeing each one as a spirit rather than a body. Or when shopping at the grocery store I would stop and just watch the shoppers. It was like a drug, but better! I reached incredible highs. Life was suddenly like a joke or a game. I knew that we were truly all actors upon the stage of life! A statement that I had heard many times but never really understood - until then. Spirits walking around in physical bodies pretending that this world was actually real! "What a concept!", I thought to myself.

Then one day, about a month later, something happened. I was in downtown Oakland on 14th and Alice watching people and I saw something that sent me into a state of depression and horror. It was just before 1:00 PM, the end of the lunch hour. I was looking at a man walking with his briefcase. He apparently had just finished eating lunch - probably a business lunch. I was looking at him as spirit and I realized something that was always there but had escaped my consciousness. He, as a spirit, was not really in the body. As he walked, his focus was so much on other things that the spirit was drifting a distance out of his body. Soon I realized that I had seen this countless times before, but had never really looked at it. But now I must. Everyone I looked at for the next hour was in a similar state: all of their energy was focused outside of themselves. Not just outside of their bodies, but outside of their awareness of self. I felt such sorrow and compassion for these people, that I didn't know how to handle it. I realized that this was the basis for my urgency for freedom all of those years. Subconsciously I knew that I was not free, but I didn't really understand, until that day, the scope of this condition in the world.

But I learned over a period of time how to handle it - how to handle the condition of the human race in this day and age. People imprisoned by the outside world; barred from the inner world of spirit - the inner world of freedom. Freedom is within and the whole world is looking for freedom outside of themselves: more money, a relationship, new house, vacations, cars, another spiritual course or book, …etc.

Freedom is an attainable state for everyone. But it is never given, it must always be earned or in reality, fought for. No one is going to hand it to or make it easy for you to be free. The nature of the world today is to control one another, to place restrictions and conditions upon everyone - especially the ones we love. People cannot give each other true freedom because of a fear of loss. Mostly the loss of love. For this reason, as you go through the process of setting yourself free, others around you may challenge you or even attempt to block your process. This is not a conscious act on their part. But regardless of them not knowing what they are doing, you must learn to do whatever is necessary to move forward, because only you can set yourself free.

Truly reaching this state of consciousness enables one to see others as they truly are: spiritual beings. This inspires true love for people and one's self. This consciousness also enables one to see the world as it truly is: a schoolhouse designed to lead the individual to self-realization as an immortal being. This brings peace and harmony to one's life and success on all levels of being because suddenly the spirit flows through all aspects of life. This heals and energizes on all levels.

Once spiritual freedom is achieved through the understanding and practice of spiritual truths, then freedom on all other levels is at hand. For me, just knowing that I am a spirit, an immortal being, brings me to a state of freedom and joy. Knowing that I am not bound by this world or this physical body is liberating on all levels: physically, mentally, emotionally and spiritually. Even financially. This is the only true freedom that I know of and I have been searching and studying this now since 1973. This has been my passion, my love and my life. All human beings must be free to truly experience the grandeur and glory of this gift of life. And it all comes down to one thing: Spirit. Once you truly know who you are, beyond any doubt, all things are possible and life becomes synonymous with joy, freedom, love and enthusiasm.

Chapter Eight

POWER OF THE WORD

There is so much happening on the planet to be aware of, but first and foremost, we must be totally aware of what is happening within ourselves. And within ourselves is like a whole world of itself. There is so much attention that is needed to be focused within. As one trains in their spiritual abilities and practices true spiritual concepts and truths on a consistent and impeccable basis, the initiate will be able to flow more easily through life, but at the same time will be always at attention, or at tension. In other words, the initiate will be relaxed but always aware of their space and the condition (or conditioning), of the space of others. Like most abilities worth acquiring, some or much practice is required in order to master the ability. With the following exercises, to be successful, you must focus and become totally impeccable at all times. You must begin to manifest what we call the warrior spirit within yourself.

The warrior spirit is an attitude and an awareness. An attitude that one is never a victim and is truly the creator of his/her personal reality. And the awareness of what in reality is the cause of the actions or the reactions that you express. It is said that we are never upset for the reasons we think. This is true. And becoming aware of how and why you are truly effected does give you the opportunity to heal that which keeps you from a state of perfect expression of health, happiness and abundance. Realize that the greatest battles are within yourself, and in reality, the only battles are within yourself. When you have conquered the enemy within, you have won all the battles. The following is one of the first steps to true power.

It has been said that silence is golden. Well, this I am sure is something that most people can agree on. Often, more has been said in silence than with words. Yet it is with words in which we most commonly communicate to one another. Until the day comes when all people have developed their telepathy to the degree in which speaking through the vocal cords is unnecessary, we must bear with the inconsistencies of human languages. Translating thoughts and ideas into words is often difficult or impossible. Any word, especially one with impact, can have a very different meaning to each individual. Particularly with different sexes. The words "love, affection, and responsibility" have similar but very different meanings to men and women. One of the biggest problems today in relationships is communication breakdown. There is no longer a meeting place with words between males and females. The gap has widened beyond hope for most. But you have the opportunity to bridge that gap for yourself in this teaching, by learning to use words more purposefully with power. Already with this small illustration, you can see how the word can have power. The ability to communicate effectively where your peers cannot is well worth acquiring. But those who communicate most effectively are those who are aware of who they truly are and have developed the ability to express their true selves consistently and consciously throughout their life.

CRITICISM: Jesus said in the Bible "It is not what goes into your mouth that defiles you, but what comes out of your mouth that defiles you." He, of course, was referring to the spoken word. Imagine, if this is true, what power the words that you so carelessly allow to flow from your lips can have on your life. Think about it. What comes out of your mouth DEFILES you. Defile is a very strong and graphic word: Filthy, dirty, unclean; those are some of the meanings. What He was meaning was that everything you say is a prayer for or against yourself. EVERYTHING YOU SAY IS A PRAYER FOR OR AGAINST YOURSELF. Let's take a look at that for just a moment... Every time you validate your fellow man or woman, you have said a prayer of validation for yourself. Every time you wish someone a happy, healthy and whole life, you say a prayer for yourself for a happy, healthy and whole life. Every time you tell someone to go to hell, you say a prayer against yourself to go to hell. Every time you say that you hope someone experiences a loss, you say a prayer against yourself hoping that you experience a loss of some sort. You see, people have become so critical, that they spend more time saying negative things about themselves and everyone else than positive statements about anything. And the negative has more power than the positive with most people, because most people expect to experience the negative rather than the positive. And the more they experience in the negative, the more faith they have in the negative, therefore the more negative they experience. And this snowballs until the individual becomes very powerful in the negative. Fortunately, these people are so unconscious (out of their body), that their power only effects themselves and not others. Somewhere along the line, this critical nature crystallizes within their space, which makes it so they are powerless against it and it becomes so much a part of them that they are not even aware that they are negative in any way, shape or form. As a matter of fact, most negative people truly believe that they are very positive and are, as they would say, "realistic". Even though they can easily see the negativity in others, they cannot (or will not) see it in themselves. That is their free will.

On the other hand, the individual that is truly positive in nature, will always find a way to validate others and him/herself. And will continue to become more and more powerful in the positive. And if the positive person does criticize him/herself or another, it is done as constructive criticism. The difference between constructive criticism and the way most people criticize is like the difference between love and hate. Both are at the same energy vibration, but opposite ends of the spectrum. Constructive criticism is used to correct and heal. Non-constructive criticism adds more negative energy to an already negative (or sometimes positive) situation. One adds to destruction and the other heals or neutralizes. The classic example of how critical energy works in your space is the person who during his/her youth always criticized his/her father or mother, and then suddenly one day realizes that he/she has become the very thing that he/she has always hated. So he has become his father, or she has become her mother; or he has become his mother, or she has become her father. It can be said that one becomes what one resists, hates or criticizes. This ensures that the individual has the opportunity to become neutral to most everything on this earth. For by becoming what one hates or resists, the individual has the perfect opportunity to see, experience and then transmute the energy first hand within his/her own space.

COMPLAINING CONSCIOUSNESS: Again, we are talking about a very destructive energy. There are many who constantly complain. Nothing seems to be good enough, or just right for these types of people. No matter where they are working, they are not happy. No matter what class they are in, there is something wrong with it, and/or they are not happy. Wherever they go or whatever they do, they usually are not happy. And they can and do always tell you many "very good reasons" why they are not happy. Do you know someone like this? I do, and I'm sure you do too. This is the person that always believes that the grass is greener on the other side. Or the one that is always saying, "if only this would happen then I would be so happy..." This is the person that is always setting conditions for his/her happiness. The one that is never satisfied with what they have or who they are.

The trouble with this kind of thinking is that the individual is always setting out-of-reach conditions for his/her happiness. In truth, anything outside yourself is an out-of-reach condition. But this is done on purpose. This person does not want to be happy. This person truly believes that he/she wants happiness, but in reality, most people are more in love with their misery and "hardships" than with the Supreme Being. You've heard the saying "misery loves company", well I have news for you, misery DEMANDS company! That is why these people constantly complain to other people. They want you to be as miserable and unhappy as them, so that you both can play victim and martyr. After all, complaining to one's self is no fun at all! There is no satisfaction in that game, so the complainer must find an accomplice or in some cases a victim. This is why so many complainers have so few real friends. When people get to know them, they don't want to be around them. It is our spiritual nature to be repelled by complaining (lower astral plane) energy.

The reason that it is repelling to spirits is that when one complains about his/her situation in life, he/she is literally slapping the Supreme Being in the face. He/she is taking what God gave to them to work with and rejecting it as no good or second rate. What you have in your life are your raw materials. You have been given more than enough to create for yourself a happy, healthy, wealthy and whole life on planet Earth. Our One Father/Mother God is a GIVING God. All He wants to do is to give, give, and give some more. But in total human ignorance, people refuse to receive and then deny what was already given to them! Can you imagine if you were a parent and every time you gave a gift to your child, he or she complained because it wasn't good enough? How long would you keep giving? Well, fortunately, the Supreme Being never stops giving. But people close up and turn away and refuse to receive. And then, as if that is not enough, they blame and/or complain to the Supreme Being for their lack of health, wealth and happiness!

Soon, the Supreme Being begins to give to the individual what it appears that the person wants. In other words, if you are always emanating low vibrational negative energy and consciousness then that is what the Supreme Being will give back to you to create with. The Supreme Being will always give what ever it is that you want, and you will always demonstrate through action what it is you really want. UNBELIEVABLE you may be thinking. Yes, I agree, utterly unbelievable! But, nonetheless true. Such PRIDE, EGO (edging God out), and VAINGLORY does truly exist within human beings. If you are around such energy, I suggest that you get away immediately until you know how to effectively transmute and purify death into life! And if you are a compulsive complainer, then now is the time to repent (rethink and radically change your ways), BEFORE you become too powerful in the negative.

WORDS HAVE POWER: Whatever you say, no matter how meaningless you think it is, has power. You are the WORD made flesh and the energy of your soul takes on an angelic quality to bring forth the DESIRED (2nd chakra) results of what you IMAGINE (6th chakra) to experience. Then by VOCALIZING (5th chakra) your desire, you open up the 3rd chakra to create a magnetic quality to DRAW to your body the experience which you have vocalized. Most people therefore, experience a negative and unhappy life as a result of their malicious critical nature towards themselves and others.

This Teaching is a course in which you learn and practice using not only your 2nd, 3rd, 5th and 6th chakras but also the 1st, 4th and 7th. Unlike most people that are "asleep", you will KNOW (7th chakra) what you desire. You will become conscious of the subconscious mind, thereby eliminating unwanted "surprises" brought about by unconscious thoughts and words. You will also have the ability to MATERIALIZE (1st chakra) the object or experience desired, rather than waiting and hoping. And you will understand how to LOVE (4th chakra) your creations, yourself and others correctly and righteously (right use of).

It will become crucially important for you to say only what you want to experience for yourself. You must, as you become more powerful, learn to tame the tongue. Your words are your prayers, and prayers do get answered sooner or later! You must mean what you say and say what you mean. You do not have to be mean about it, just mean it! Be totally conscious of every word that passes your lips and how those words may effect you some day. Sooner or later, everything you say will come back to visit you in a way in which you may least expect or enjoy! Words and thoughts form. You've heard the term "thought form"? Well thoughts do form. And words form even faster. Your thoughts and words are like little angels that go out and do your bidding for you. And sooner or later, they find whatever it is you are or were mocking up and bring it to you like good little servants. Yes, servants. Your thoughts and words are

59

suppose to serve you, not control you as with most people. They are to enlighten you and others around you. But, unfortunately most are controlled by their thoughts and have no control over what comes out of their mouth most of the time.

There are specific steps to obtaining true power. First, you must realize that you have the most profound effect on your life. What happens to you is literally within your own control. The easiest way to change or improve your state in life is through your words. On one hand, it sounds too simple, and on the other hand it seems too difficult. It is hard to except that every time you say "I can't afford it" that you are creating more situations in which you will not be able to afford something. Or when you say, "I am too tired", that you are just programming yourself to be even more tired at some time in the future. To have true power in the word, to have the ability to manifest what you say in the positive, or to literally become a modern day prophet, you must first clean up your act. Become aware of every word that passes your lips. Every negative statement erases a little more of your true power. Therefore, you must eliminate what is draining you and then build upon a new foundation for true power through the word.

TAME THE TONGUE: As you grow and unfold spiritually, your fifth chakra will become more and more powerful in the sense that what you say will begin to happen sooner. The little angels called words and thoughts are already becoming more powerful. Where you are at today is a direct result of your own perspective. What you see is what you talk about, and what you see and say is what you get. You got what you saw, so now see what you saw and see what you said, and see what you got. If you want a better life than what you got, then all you need to do is simply TAME THE TONGUE. Once you get control of the tongue, controlling the thoughts will be much easier. You see, the thoughts control the tongue, so therefore if you take away the tongue, the thoughts cannot express themselves without your SUPER-VISION. And when your vision is super, then you can watch the thoughts and see exactly where they originate. Once you know where they are coming from, like which chakra, or possibly some other spirit, then you the spirit can begin to take control of your thoughts and words and life. AMEN!!

EXERCISE: It has been said that silence is golden. This is true. How true it is you will discover first hand. This exercise is to spend one day this next week, in total silence. Total silence means absolutely no communication whatsoever on any level. At the end of your day in silence, write down your experiences and realizations.

In addition, from this moment on and for the next four weeks, do not in any way, shape or form, complain or criticize to anyone. Keep a small notebook with you and write down any complaint or criticism that passes your lips during these weeks. At the end of the four weeks, study this list and you will discover where it is you are vulnerable to negative speaking. This may require a great deal of will power for you. But, if you can accomplish these two simple exercises, you may have some amazing experiences and realizations. If you do not complain or criticize for the entire four weeks, your whole life will change for the better. But don't take my word for it - try it!

Chapter Nine

THE GOD PERSPECTIVE

In this day and age, there is an abundance of Psychics in the world. As a matter of fact, psychics are a dime a dozen. The old belief that clairvoyance is a special gift has pretty much been destroyed in many areas of the world. And this is the way it should be. Psychic gifts or spirituals, are not something that one should be in awe of. In reality, the state of constant and total awareness is the natural state for us to be in. To be unaware and asleep is a state in which we had to work at for many years to achieve. This state of sleep now seems so natural to the vast majority of the population that when one awakens, he or she is viewed as some sort of an oddity, or in very many minds a threat to society.

The topic of this chapter is "PERSPECTIVE". But there is more to this than meets the eye. There are many ways to perceive or to not perceive. Eventually, everyone will awaken and everyone will see or, in other words, become "psychic". This is really just a matter of becoming aware that one is already aware. When this happens now days to most people, because they are so negative, they become what we call a "psickic" rather than a psychic. The question is, "Which direction will you take?" Seems like the choice is quite clear and simple, yet things are not always as they seem. What you do with what you have and with what you receive will determine whether you will be a Psychic or a Psickic. In reality, we are all psychic anyway. Whether we add the psickic to our psychic is the crucial choice.

Everyone seems to have their own perspectives on things. It is amazing when counseling couples how they each can tell me about the same event and it will sound like two completely different stories. Or how one thing is heaven to one person and hell to another. Yet it is the same thing. Which perspective is true? Here we have opposing viewpoints - or really, points from which we view life and undoubtedly, the world. And this "point of view" can make all the difference in the world in regards to how you see the world. For instance, if you were standing on the corner of Kearny and California in downtown San Francisco, the view would look much different than the view from the Carnelian Room, which is at the same corner, but about 65 floors higher. You see, perspective is based upon point of view. \par

Our motto at the Foundation for Spiritual Freedom is "SPIRIT IS FREE". But that is not entirely true. It is more of an affirmation than a statement of fact. Spirits are free in the beginning and up to a certain point after they incarnate into a physical body. But then something happens. Because of many factors, spirits in bodies begin to give up their own freedom. And very soon, by the time their bodies are eight or nine years of age they've "sold out" much of their freedom and their individuality. Somehow, little by little, the spirit becomes involved in flesh, in emotions, in personality and in human love. All of these concepts tend to imprison the spirit, because all of a sudden there are all kinds of rules and regulations. For example, certain parts of the body are "private", "dirty" or "nasty". This of course is absurd, but it still happens, even today. And it is all because they do not understand their own bodies.

Ignorance of self has imprisoned the societies of incarnated spirits on this planet. Little by little, people are programmed and conditioned to see the world in a certain light, (or darkness). This has a crippling and devastating effect on the human soul. But nothing changes, it just

63

Michael C. Fikaris

continues on and on. And because of people's own chicken-shit attitudes and perspective towards life that say "life is just a burden that we all must bare", this sick dis-ease is passed down from generation to generation. Family traditions have become more important than spiritual freedom, independence and individuality. These old ways of living encourages a sick and diseased perspective. But this can change. As you break through the shackles and chains of human programming and ignorance, you will begin to lay a new foundation for your own spiritual freedom.

What promotes this kind of diseased thinking and behavior is an unhealed perspective. Because of hypnosis, mind control and programming, people live in the worst kind of hell imaginable. A hell that is so perfectly constructed that it cannot be discerned by the vast majority of its inmates. A hell that on the surface looks so appealing and so beautiful that most fight to stay there, not knowing that they are fighting for their own poverty, misery, pain and ultimate death. Even in death there is no honor for these pathetic souls. Dying in ways that are far beneath our human dignity as Sons and Daughters of God. People dying of hunger, cancer, aids or suicide. What kind of a transition is that into the spirit world? The way people live and die reflects directly upon their consciousness and their consciousness reflects directly upon their perspective. In other words, if you see the world as an evil, threatening, limiting place, then life becomes a burden and you become a victim of circumstances rather than a Master of Life. What you see is what you get. How do you see the world? That is easy to know - just look at the quality of your thoughts. As you practice your non-complaining and non-criticizing exercises described in the Power of the Word chapter, then you will notice quite clearly the quality of your thoughts - which are a direct result of your perspective. As you

64

perceive (see), you think; as you think, you speak; and as you speak, you manifest. Heal your perspective and your world changes.

Becoming psychic is only part of the healing. If your perspective is negative (unhealed), then as the world opens up to you, you will see everything that is evil. But if your perspective is positive (healed), then you will see everything that is good. But the healed perspective can see the evil as well as the good, yet not be affected by the evil that he/she sees. In contrast, the perspective that is unhealed can only focus upon the evil in the world and is only affected by the evil that he/she sees and is virtually unaffected by the good that is always present.

Life is a GIFT. What more can the Creator give to It's Children than the gift of Life? An opportunity to learn, to play, to feel and most of all, to Love. The gift of Life is a very special gift indeed. There are countless beings within the Earth's atmosphere (aura), that wish they could have a body to experience themselves in physical form. But for some reason or another they cannot obtain a body. Yet the beings that do have bodies here spend some seventy years abusing and killing the very body that they longed for when in the spirit world. They treat their bodies horribly, filling themselves up with guilt, fear, anxiety, hatred, jealousy and competition. They torture their body until it finally gives up and dies.

People call themselves human beings, but they are rarely being humane. And ironically, they treat themselves worse than everyone else. This is called the Golden Rule: "Do unto others as you would have them do unto you." What this is really saying is do unto others as you do unto you - which is why people treat each other so shitty. Think about it - how can someone truly love someone else if they can't even love themselves? This is like teaching someone how to read when they do not even know their ABC's. So what people do is they use their energy to get someone else to love them for them. In the meantime, they are giving away all of their life force energy to some other spirit, and that is one of the things that makes bodies get sick and grow old and die. All this is done out of a sick perspective of self.

There are as many perspectives as there are people. These various perspectives are mostly based upon past time experiences, programming, prejudice, desires, fears, ambition ... etc. Each views the world from his or her own point of view. If you are a Minister, then you will look at the world much differently than a General of the Israeli army. But even though virtually everyone sees the same things differently to one degree or another, the fact of the matter is that there is only one true perspective. This may sound limiting to you, but when the Supreme Being looks at a car, He sees a mode of transportation. When we look at a car, we see status, price, comfort, color, sex appeal, speed and so on. In other words, our perspective of life, the world and the things in it, is jaded and influenced by many different factors that make us to one degree or another un-neutral to whatever we are looking at.

Here is a little story, (imagine that you are reading this in an Indian accent): Once there were four blind men, and they were sitting with their spiritual Teacher. The four blind men wanted to know what an elephant looked like. So the Master led them to a nearby neighbor who possessed an elephant. When they arrived he instructed the four blind men to walk to the elephant and feel the elephant in order to see what an elephant looks like. The first blind man grabbed a hold of the elephant's trunk and ran his hands up and down the trunk over and over again. The second blind man approached the elephant from the side and explored the massive body of the elephant. The third blind man discovered one of the elephant's front legs, which he stretched his arms around. And the forth blind man found the elephant's tail, which he held and switched back and forth several times. Eventually the Teacher called the four blind men over to him and asked each what does the elephant looked like. The first blind man said, "the elephant is like a large snake with no teeth that is very strong and can wrap around you". Suddenly, the second blind man spoke up and said "No! No! The elephant is very big like the side of a barn!" "No! No! No! My blind friends!" said the third blind man, "The elephant is like a tree trunk, round and sturdy and low to the ground!" Now at this point the fourth blind man was very angry and was shouting, "You are all crazy! You are all crazy! The elephant is like a rope, small, round and very thin! What is the matter with you?!" The blind men continued their quarrel for quite some time before the Master intervened. When the Master finally quieted everyone down, one by one he told each blind man that he was correct in his description of the elephant. "How could this be?" asked the first blind man, "We have all described very different things!". The Teacher explained that what they had described was accurate but that there was one problem, each of their perspectives, although correct, were limited. They hadn't explored the entire elephant and therefore did not get the whole picture. They were each influenced by the small amount of information that they had and by their own limited experiences, thus creating four totally different perspectives of the same elephant. Therefore, their individual realities were different.

It is a matter of perspective. Like the blind men, people's perspectives are limited. The reality you create is based upon how you see. Past experiences leave impressions that influence your perspective. And one little thing from your past or from your subconscious mind can create a world that you may not really want or need. Thus, the importance of healing your perspective. See where your perspective is negative (sick) in any way and then resolve it, (heal it). To heal your perspective, you must learn to see the entire picture and to see the true reality.

Of course, you may follow the path of so many others - the path of denial. You may continue to pretend that you do not see. You may continue to see less than God in yourself and others. You may continue to fight for your limitations. Or, you can become responsible for your own life and what you have created and truly heal your sick and distorted perspective that dictates lack, pain, fear and misery.

For some people, there is a day of reckoning. Then for a few of those people, a day of repentance (a change in ways). This is where you can be today. You, who are reading these words on these pages, may have already reached the day of reckoning if you so choose. A day when you recognize that what you have done so far didn't really work. Or maybe you recognized that there is more to life than rent, taxes and death. Or maybe you realized that you aren't "just human" after all. Or maybe you are becoming aware that your perception of the world may not be exactly the way the world is. Or that maybe someone you trusted long ago lied to you and that particular lie is still lying in your space, possibly right in front of your sixth chakra, coloring your perspective so that you see things in a certain light. Whatever the story, your story, you are here now. And everything in your past, as insignificant as it might seem, has led you to this time and place to read these words on these pages and to now become aware that you are aware and are rapidly becoming more aware all the time. To now realize that your day of reckoning has come. Maybe you now know who you are, what you are and where you are. Or maybe, you are realizing that there is more to you than meets the eye, such as a wealth of power. The question is, what are you going to do with it?

"What to do" in deed is the question! And do with WHAT might just be your next question. The answer to WHAT is easy - knowledge. There is an old saying, "A little knowledge is dangerous." Just think what a lot of knowledge can do! Knowledge can elevate the individual to greatness. But if it has the power to elevate, it too has the power to sink the individual into utter darkness. What you do with what you have will make all the difference between you and the thousands that have walked a similar path, but failed along the way.

Your perspective of the world, yourself, and others will dictate what you will do with your acquired knowledge and abilities. So many psychics have become psickics because of their misuse of knowledge (power). Because they were caught up in their own vainglory, pride and ego, they have wasted and squandered their power to rule over others rather than help and heal those in need. It is all a matter of perspective. They would rather "rule in hell than to serve in Heaven". Yet, the greatest angels in Heaven are those who serve. What you do with your new found power is entirely up to you, no one will interfere with your learning lessons or your free will. But I urge you to rise to the level of one who sees God in everything and everyone and then you may be raised to the level of one who serves. It is all a matter of perspective.

I will end this chapter with a story from the Bible, Luke 22:27: The Disciples were discussing who among them would be the greatest in Heaven. And Jesus said to them, "For who is greater, he who sits at the table, or he who serves? Is it not he who sits at the table? Yet, I am among you as the One who serves." It is all perspective…

Chapter Ten

PROGRAMMING

As clairvoyants, when we speak of programming, we are speaking of the information that we have collected in one way or another that tells our personality what is right and wrong, good and bad, funny and serious, loving and hateful, and beautiful and ugly. (Of course the list does go on.) This programming is what makes our bodies and personalities react in a certain way in any given situation. This information is also known to psychics as "mental image pictures". There are many different aspects of programming. It is important to become aware of the various degrees of programming that you and mostly all other human beings are operating on while on this planet. The programming that is not your own must at some time be eliminated and replaced with your own spiritual programming. This is absolutely essential as you walk along your path of self-realization. A major part of realizing who you are is first realizing who you are not. Most people identify with aspects of their personality that have been transferred to them from other people early in life. Much or even most of this programming may not work well. The problem is that until it is identified and brought into conscious awareness, it goes unnoticed and unhealed causing havoc on many levels.

Bear in mind that not all programming is "bad" or "negative". Some of the programming that you have inherited, or picked up along the way is very valid and useful. The big fear that many people have is being "programmed by someone". Well the truth of the matter is that all people are programmed already, much more than they could ever imagine. And the majority of this programming was done to them by other people. So their fears have already materialized, but they are so programmed that they do not even realize this. In fact, most are programmed to believe that they are not programmed at all and that they are truly independent and free thinkers... HELLO!

BODY PROGRAMMING:

The truth is that you are not the body. You have probably heard this before, but do you actually believe it? And if you do believe it, have you actually realized it? Knowing something intellectually and realizing it in your life are two entirely different things. The realization of a thing dictates action based upon that information which has been realized. Therefore there is a change not only in understanding but also in behavior and action. Again, realize that you are not the body. The body is merely a vehicle of expression. An object in which we can experience ourselves in physical form; at best, a learning tool. And this three-dimensional world is just a training ground for spirits. Training for what, you might ask. Well, that is another chapter... The point is, that your physical body is very much like the car you drive in. What is funny, is that most people take better care of their car than they do their body - yet they believe that they are the body. What does THAT tell you about the condition (or conditioning) of the human mind? Like a car, without you, the body is just a hunk of matter. It needs you to start it up and keep it running. Without you, there is no life in the body at all. The body is literally nothing without the spirit. Life force is channeled only through the spirit - not directly to the body.

71

Michael C. Fikaris

Those who spend so much time healing the body are wasting their time. Heal the spirit and the mind and then the body will heal.

The best way to keep the body alive and running is to love it. By "love", I mean using and treating the body correctly. Not loving other bodies and trying to get them to love mine for me, but loving mine and allowing them to love their own and maybe we will have love between us. I love my body by letting it be a body, which means to me letting my body do the five things a body likes to do - BREATHE, EAT, SLEEP, MATE, AND ELIMINATE. I also love my body by treating it to meditation and consciously giving it light and love.

The deepest layer of body programming is the genetic programming. This is the programming that you inherited in the body from thousands of years of genetic information being passed down from generation to generation. As the programming was passed down from generation to generation, it became stronger. The more dominant genes became even more dominant and the weaker genes were phased out over the centuries. If your body is a pure bred, meaning that there are no other mixtures of race or nationality within your body, then the programming is that much more powerful.

What the ancestral genetic programming dictates is the foods that the body likes to eat, the types of bodies it likes to mate with, the overall structure of the body and the emotional state of the body, (remember that the emotions are an expression of the body).

As a spirit, you were given your biological parents because of their vibration, consciousness and genetic make up. You needed their programming in order to fulfill your destiny on this planet. By looking at what you received from them, you can take what is needed now and transmute the rest. As spirits of the Aquarian Age, it is your task to take the old and transmute it to the new higher vibration, whether good or bad. Therefore, the physical programming must be consciously worked upon.

To accomplish this, try the following exercise: Sit totally naked in front of a full length mirror for 45 minutes per day in a meditative state with your eyes open. Then gaze at your body and you will begin to see programming, energy patterns and blocks around the different parts of the body. You may be able to identify where the energy came from originally, like your mother or father. And you may also receive information about how that programming effects your life. When you identify the energy, do not worry so much about how or why, just focus on the energy draining down into the ground. At the end of your 45 minute session, send love to every part of the body and watch how it responds to the love.

THE FOOD HABIT:

All bodies like to eat. Different bodies like different foods. Most of what people put in their bodies is a direct result of ancestral programming. Even if the individual has drifted away from their family eating habits and has become a vegetarian, you will find that there are still remains of that ancestral programming that will dictate the kind of fruits and vegetables the person likes and how he/she likes the food prepared. As the body is transmuted of course, all this can be changed.

The amount of food people put into their bodies is also a matter of programming. In truth, these bodies do not need any food whatsoever. Yes, that is what I said, these bodies do not need any food whatsoever. They have the ability to manufacture everything that they need to keep the body

Michael C. Fikaris

strong and healthy and young. These bodies in reality are self-contained units (in their pure form). The reason that our bodies must eat in this day and age is a direct result of genetic programming. In the beginning, human beings only ate a small amount of fruit. The purpose of this was only to cleanse the body. To help keep the system clean by eliminating impurities that the body might pick up. The necessity to eat foods that would build the body up or give the body energy, was nonexistent in those days. But after the fall of man, human beings became more animal like. When their consciousness dropped, they lost their ability to transmute energy and energize the body and began to eat small amounts of food, such as nuts and grains for fuel in the body. As they began to eat more heavier foods, it took more energy to digest. Soon, humans began to require sleep to rest and re-energize. Just like a junkie, the more they ate, the more they needed to eat to keep the bodies going. And the more they ate the heavier and denser the bodies became. Also, like the female junkie that is pregnant, the addiction for food was passed down from generation to generation and became more and more powerful with each passing generation. And now, here we are in present time. We live in a society where there is more food than we know what to do with. People are today eating twenty times the amount of food that they need to fuel the body. Gluttony is rampant. And just like the junkies, people are eating when they celebrate, when they are emotional, when they are nervous and mostly just out of habit. Whether they are hungry or not, most people will eat a set number of meals at set times each day. And it is this very addiction that contributes to the body growing old, becoming ill and getting tired.

These bodies are so programmed for food that it is a great task to get this particular habit under control. Since 1982, I have studied myself and others during meals. The most striking thing that I have learned is that most people are no where near their bodies during feeding times. This may sound contrary at first, but let's take a look at it. When I say out of their body, I mean unconscious. Not conscious of what they are doing. Most people are chit-chatting around the table, watching TV or reading something. And if none of those, than they will be deep in thought about someone or some problem or some project. In other words, people eat by rote, automatically and excessively. During the feeding, they experience at times almost a sensual like feeling. When they are done, they feel a satisfaction, a glow, very much like an addict after a couple of drinks or a fix. They are aware of the first few bites of food because that is all the body really needs, then their attention strays, and within minutes they have unconsciously devoured an excessive amount of substance.

There was a study several years ago in which doctors took a group of babies and fed them the standard approved diet. And at the same time took another group and allowed them to choose their own diet by just laying out a variety of different foods. After a few months they discovered that the infants that chose their own foods were brighter, stronger, and had virtually no physical illness' in that period of time. And they found that those babies consistently chose fruit for almost every meal. On the other hand, the other group had all the common diseases and problems that most other babies have.

Fruit. Fruit is what they ate almost always. Whenever you start to give an infant vegetables and meat, the first thing they do is spit it out! But they LOVE fruit. Just maybe, children know more about what is good for the body than adults do. After all, they more recently crossed over from the spirit world.

Michael C. Fikaris

Most of my children have been raised for the first couple years of their lives here on almost all fruit and small amounts of grain. They have all been raised as vegetarians with little dairy. All of them are bright and extremely healthy. Most of them have never been to a doctor and possibly never will. The others have not been more than two or three times. Also, there are a few of us who have brought our food consumption down to only two or three days a week for years at a time. The other four or five days a week were/are spent only consuming distilled water, fruit and fruit juice. Accomplishing this has been a gradual process and our goal is to become totally non-dependent upon foods - breatharians. But this takes time. The body must slowly adjust and begin to manufacture on it's own the necessary proteins and nutrients to keep it healthy. This is mostly done through extracting these things from the air that we breathe and through meditation. Currently, we are experiencing more health and energy than ever before.

Now, DO NOT go out and change your diet!! I mean that. Just take a look. Begin to become more conscious during meals. Be totally aware of each and every bite of food that goes into your body. Be aware of when the body NEEDS food, rather than when you want to eat. Become more aware of why you are eating most of the time. I am not trying to preach fruitarianism or breatharianism. I am here just to open your eyes a bit. We are talking about many thousands of years of addiction/programming in that body, so if you do anything at all, do it SLOWLY. Spend a few years at it and the transmutation will last.

MATING GAME:

Since this book is not specifically about relationships, I will keep this aspect of body programming to a minimum.

Basically, the body has a procreative urge. This urge used to be, at one time, satisfied through sexual activity. It is absolutely necessary to have this urge. Without it the human race would die off. In it's pure form, this urge is creative, therefore female in nature and in principle. Through the act of mating, the Supreme Being has given to us the most pleasurable experience the body can ever have. Of course, I am talking about sex without games or addiction. Without pride, ego, possession and control, sex is almost the most wonderful experience on the planet. It is the second most driving force in human nature. The programming that I want you to look at here is any that says sex is dirty, nasty or ugly. You should be the only one that has the power to restrict your body from partaking in any form of pain or pleasure. Your body is YOUR body. No one has the right to tell you what to do with your body. If someone does not like what you are doing, then they have the right to leave or remove themselves from your space. There is no room for judgment of any form concerning the sexual activities of anyone. Freedom IS what freedom GIVES.

On the other hand, because of incorrect understanding of sex throughout the ages, people have come to misunderstand sex and it's correct uses. Therefore, there is a lot of sexual misuse throughout the world. As a matter of fact, sexual misuse is rampant. What this does to people, is eliminates the possibility for them to derive from sex the healing that it was meant to bring. So people today are mostly sexually frustrated or unhappy and are rarely truly satisfied. It is safe to say that this condition includes a vast majority of the population. What causes this, is negative programming about sex. That could include anything from "Sex is bad, dirty and nasty" to "Sex is the end-all and getting laid at any cost is the most important thing in life". Being addicted to sex is just as bad as being sexually closed

77

down. Both situations are destructive to the body, mind and soul. Using sex correctly will heal and expand one's consciousness to heights that are unimaginable. But sexual power and control games eliminate these possibilities, and turn this powerful energy against your good.

You will discover any and all sex games within and without your space as you go through this teaching. I do recommend one thing, from this day on, you may want to begin to uncover what is dirty, nasty or ugly under the covers. This topic is the most sensitive and runs the deepest with just about every body/personality. Most everyone is hung up on sex and love. The problem is that if you have sexual programming that is creating sexual blocks, then you also have creative blocks that are hindering you from creating the life that you truly desire. I recommend that you check and transmute your programming around this issue until you feel that it is totally healed.

SLEEPING:

As I mentioned above, the body likes to sleep. And then I said that the body needs to sleep. Well, both are true. Any reformed addict will tell you that he/she liked and needed their addiction. The same holds true for the body. As the bodies through time became gross and more dense, the spirits needed to get out of the body to do effective healing work on them. So what happens when the body goes to sleep, is that you slip out into an astral body to do whatever healing work you can. People could not any longer keep their bodies clean of lower vibrational energies, so they had to do it unconsciously. And as people became more unconscious spiritually, the more physical sleep they needed. "As above so below", right? The amount of sleep reflected how asleep they were and are. As time went on, sleep became more than just a necessity, but an enjoyment. People, especially recently, have become less active and sleep longer. You always hear people say that they never get enough sleep. This just enhances the situation.

As you walk along your path, and your energy vibration increases, and your meditations become more effective, you will find that your body requires less sleep. The reason for this is because you will be doing most of the work consciously rather than unconsciously. You the spirit never sleeps. Even the subconscious mind never sleeps. But, what keeps you from keeping your body awake is your subconscious mind. As you clean out your subconscious mind and make it conscious, then you will have more control over your body/personality. On the other hand, working on programming is the most difficult subject to stay awake for. Programming is a form of hypnosis, which is a form of sleep. You had to go to sleep, or forget your divinity, to allow yourself to be programmed. As the programming and hypnosis comes up in your space, you may experience the sleep as it is coming out. As unconscious energy comes out of your space, the body thinks it is time to go to sleep because it feels the unconscious energy. But once you go through that energy and release it, then you have broken through a layer of unconscious energy and you have become more conscious then before. More awake then you were moments ago. Eventually, you will no longer need more than a couple of hours of sleep per week. Maybe even less, depending upon where you live.

The programming that we have discussed so far has mostly come through and from your parents. You see, no matter how rebellious people were as teenagers, as they got older they became their parents programming. Dad became Grandpa and Mom became Grandma. As kids and teenagers it is easy to rebel because the body's vibration is too high at that time to house the lower vibration of the parents. But as the body gets older and slows down a bit or burns out, then that deep seeded programming begins to come alive. Begins to take over the body/personality. And soon there is no fighting it. At this point, most people give up and accept the fact that they are just like their parents.

For those on the path of self-realization, there is a different story to tell. The first thing the budding initiate sees is his/her parents everywhere in his/her space. And of course, everyone else's parents in their space too. This of course, is natural since this is the most dominant program. So, as you the student neutralizes the parental programming in your space, you may find that your parents will act up from time to time. There are many reasons for this: 1. They are getting their energy back from your space; 2. This energy is purified by you before it is sent back, therefore it is at a much higher vibration; 3. On a spirit level they know that you are destroying the program and breaking a link in the genetic chain. That makes it hard for them to find another body sometime in the future with similar genetic and ancestral programming. You see, chances are that your parents had plans to get a body someday from one of YOUR grandchildren. It's like playing leapfrog. That is one of the main reasons (unconsciously) why parents get upset with their children when they do not have children of their own.

Working on your programming is a task that is on going. Every cell in your body, down to the marrow of your bones, is programmed. There is much more than meets the eye. We haven't even talked about religion, politics and death programming. Never stop de-programming and always become more aware of what and who is programming you in present time. These bodies are like computers, they must run on a program of some sort - just make sure it is yours!

Exercise:

The exercise for this chapter may at first seem difficult for you, but I assure you that it can be accomplished very easily if you make a true decision to do it. Like all of the exercises in this book, it is YOU who will benefit from this assignment… IF you do it correctly as given. The exercise is as follows: Seven days of fruit and fruit juice only. Eat nothing but fresh fruit and drink nothing but fruit juice. The details are as follows: no dried fruit; no fruit with vegetable properties (such as tomatoes); only one avocado and one banana per day, if at all; have as much citrus as possible including fresh squeezed juices whenever possible; exercise daily, but do not overwork yourself physically; meditate as often as possible; always have some fresh fruit with you to satisfy cravings; when drinking water, use only distilled.

If this exercise is done correctly, you will find an increase in energy and awareness, and at the same time you will have the opportunity to blow a lot of pictures. If you have a lot of will power at your disposal, I recommend only distilled water for the last 1-3 days. If you do only water these last days, then add to one gallon of distilled water the juice of 4 squeezed lemons, 1/4 teaspoon of cayenne pepper and 2 table spoons of black strap molasses. This will give you grounding, energy and aid in the cleansing process.

Michael C. Fikaris

Chapter Eleven

HOLIDAY HOLOCAUST
THE DEATH OF CHRISTMAS

What does the holiday season bring up for you? What does it really mean for you when Christmas approaches? I see my children and the excitement in their eyes as we talk about Christmas and Santa Claus and all the magic that is connected to it. It is a wonderful thing as an adult to be reminded of the true meaning of Christmas and the way it was intended long ago. The purity, the joy, and of course, the fun. I remember as a child the joy of shopping for relatives and the excitement I felt as they opened their gifts from me. What a healing! Yes, it was nice to receive, but the true thrill was in the giving.

I still remember when they tried to murder Santa Claus in my mind. I was quite young actually when they told me that Santa did not really exist - 6 years old. Luckily I was too young to believe them. I knew the truth, that Santa did exist in reality, and that no one could really kill him. I didn't understand exactly how it worked, but I was definitely not fooled by this evil and sadistic act. I often wonder how many parents today have become so jaded and negative about life that they feel compelled to kill the magic in their children by murdering Santa? Too many, I am sure.

Now that I understand much more of life and the true meaning of Santa and Christmas, it is easy to keep them both alive within myself and my children. At the same time, my heart goes out to all the people in the world who's faith is being slaughtered every year at this time - especially the children who so innocently look to their parents for

82

guidance and understanding of life. What a shame to kill life in this way.

Christmas and Santa Claus is about the Christ. About the Christ in all His many names, shapes and forms. It is about the gift of life and the reality of the Universe for each and every human being. It is about sharing the beauty, the glory and the grandeur of this paradise planet and the Universe, with others. And, it is not about just one day per year, but about every day, every year.

Who killed Christmas? Who killed Santa? That is easy: the same people that tried to kill the Christ in Jesus. The same ones that killed your hope, love and happiness. The same ones that say to you to "keep your feet on the ground and live in reality", THEIR reality, that is. This is a slaughter that has been going on since the beginning of time. It starts in childhood. At some point, a child is "taught" about the "facts of life" - or about the "harsh realities" of life. This comes subtly for most children through their parent's negative attitudes about life. Sometimes, it comes obviously through direct conversation in which the parent plainly tells the child that life is hard and there is not hope but to survive. Statements like: "You usually do not get what you want. Nothing comes easy in life. Don't live in a fantasy world. The real world is a cruel and hard place. You work your whole life just to survive and then you die. Life is a burden... etc." (Sound familiar?)

Then there are the churches. They "innocently" portray Jesus as a weak martyr who suffered, was tortured and was killed. The man who had the power to channel the Christ and stand up to all of society in those days, was supposed to have been tormented. They ignore his strength that is repeatedly demonstrated throughout the bible and focus on and reinforce the negatives: the rejection, the torture, the crucifixion, the fear in Gethsemane and so on.

83

Michael C. Fikaris

Then of course, is this scientific mentality that has been programmed into the minds of the world. An extremely limiting way of perceiving life and reality. A system which demands absolute proof for everything that exists. Without proof, according to this mentality, it does not exist. Because of this huge step backwards in our evolution as a race of people, much has been lost. We are now taught that "seeing is believing". If you can't see it, then you cannot believe in it… If you can't prove it, it does not exist. But what about love? Can anyone see love? Can anyone prove it actually exists? They say that you can FEEL love. Well, is that enough proof? I guess so, for many. What if I told you that I can feel the Christ? Or I can feel the magic of Santa Claus? Does that make it real then? Or does that make me crazy? What about all the children in the world that KNOW Santa exists? Many say that they have seen him. What are they seeing?

Fortunately, science will eventually prove spirituality. Already, quantum physics accepts that there are many realities, and that reality is constantly changing. "Anything is possible" is no longer just a positive affirmation - it is reality. What we see in the world is a very personal experience. Our perspectives and beliefs dictate what we see and experience. Reality for each of us is literally created from this point of view. Does that mean that Santa is real for just those who believe and not for those who don't? Yes.

Who can prove otherwise? No one yet has proven that Santa or the Christ does not exist. Nor have they proven that love truly exists. The same holds true for the existence of God. Either way, not proven. Yet, every culture in the world has their own concept of God, of Jesus, of the Christ, and even of the great flood. All acts of faith. All standing the test of time. All a reality for those people.

Next we have the greed factor. Beginning with the corporations who have systematically turned Christmas into a multi-billion dollar industry. A reality now where the most important thing is buying a good enough gift for the ones you love. This translates subconsciously into "show your love by your gift". And then into "show me you love me by your gift to me". Now, there are a couple of generations of people who only think and care about what they are going to GET rather then GIVE for Christmas. The problem with this consciousness is obvious. Of course, this is not a problem for the corporations - more of a solution, really. Think about it, the advertising at Christmas time is directed to who? The parents or the children? The children. Are they taught to give? No. They are shown the things that they are made to want for themselves. This creates a "me" or an "I want" consciousness. Then the child nags the parent for the things that they want and they usually get them.

Eventually, the child grows up with great expectations and becomes even more demanding. Unfortunately, this personality habit pattern does not change and Christmas becomes often a depressing time of year. Because of the above mentioned programming, plus the deeper false programming about this holiday, relationships are often strained during the Christmas season. The true joy of the Christmas or Christ spirit is lost. The magic and simplicity is gone and expectations are high. Adults create a fantasy in their minds about what a perfect Christmas must be like. This fantasy often involves love or, actually romance, certain gifts that express certain things, types of foods, an environment, and specific interactions with other people. The whole season from before Thanksgiving though New Years is a living hell for many people. Obligations are overwhelming, the tension is building and time is running out. People are blackmailing each other and every one knows it, yet no one does anything about it. Playing the game either becomes unconscious, or tolerated for fear of rejection.

Thus, the Holiday Holocaust. Every year, many are killed, a little at a time. The false love, the greed, the frustration, and the brutal death of Santa brings about this tragedy. Santa's death symbolizes the death of the spirit of giving and the hope for the future. An all loving and giving being is destroyed or sometimes ruthlessly used to control the children's behavior. Reality is being twisted into a poisonous manipulation, all in the name of Christmas.

Yet, it is still most people's favorite time of the year. The excitement of receiving for many is worth the trouble. There are still those who love to give, but really don't know how, so they give on December 25th. It is easy. There are those who only connect with family during Christmas day. For them, it is a special time as well. And there are a few, very few, who still remember what Christmas is all about. They are the ones who become Santa, bringing love, life and joy into everyone's lives. These are the ones that do not expect or want anything for Christmas, just the opportunity to give of themselves, because they truly know that it is more blessed to give than it is to receive. And they know that the greatest gift lies within themselves: the gift of magic, of love and of life.

Chapter Twelve

CONQUERING DEATH

Everyone at some point in time during their life on planet Earth has fantasized about the death of their body. Many people have done this quite often and regularly. In most cases these people are fantasizing about the death of themselves, as if they actually can die. They are unaware that they are not the body and they really believe that they can die. Quite often, people feel that they cannot cope with their present life or problems and hope that death will be a way out of a bad situation, or a release from the constant pain that they have experienced thus far in life.

To these people, who look forward to physical death, life is just a burden that must be borne. Suffering and unhappiness is the way of life for them, and for many of the people they know. Their true desire is to someday die in peace. To others, dreaming about death is like dreaming about a movie. People fantasize about what is going to happen after death, who will be at their funeral, and what people's reactions will be when they hear of the loss of a loved one. Will they truly miss the presence of the departed one, and have fond memories of such a lovable person? And what will be said at the funeral? For many, these imaginings bring some sort of comfort, maybe through the realization that there are people that love them and will miss them.

What is death? Death is many things to many people: mysterious, frightening, painful, sad, violent and often slow. In reality, death is nothing more than something returning to it's original essence. For the body, it is returning to energy and matter. You, the spirit, took your energy, life-force

87

Michael C. Fikaris

energy and created a body. So in order to take your energy with you, you must somehow transmute that body back into energy. Virtually all people kill their body at some point in time, then let it decompose over an extended period of time. As it decomposes, they collect their energy a little at a time. The smart ones cremate the body, thereby getting back their life-force energy much faster. The not so smart ones have their body put into one of those metal lined, sometimes air tight caskets and then buried six feet under where it will surely take a couple of centuries to decompose. This just prolongs the process of returning to original essence.

If you look around, you will see that the non-use of anything is a sort of death. The USE of a thing is what gives it life. For instance, a chair is not chair of itself, it has no consciousness of being a chair. It is our use of it as a chair that gives it life as a chair. Until it is used as a chair, it is just some material substances joined together. There is no life to anything without the spirit and spirit is energy and energy is God and God is Light and Light is E=mc 2, which is the all of everything.

Through non-use and/or incorrect use, the body begins to die. To keep the body alive, the spirit must USE the body CORRECTLY. To do this the spirit that co-created the body must spend time IN the body, and run energy through the body. The lack of flow of energy is one of the main things that causes the body to age and eventually die. Here the term "Use it or lose it" does apply. Use does not mean abuse. Abuse is just as deadly as non-use. Most people abuse their bodies until about the age of thirty to forty and then they make the transition to non-use.

Addictions, as I am sure you know, is another killer of the body. The problem with addiction is that people always become addicted to the things that are "poison" to the body. That element is what makes the addictive substance addictive. There are only a few exceptions to this rule. Most addictive energies and substances will burnout or harm the body and the mind. This applies not only to obvious substance addictions, such as drugs, alcohol, etc., but also to addictive energies and many of our basic excepted practices in modern life.

Human love is one of the deadliest addictions of all. More life-force energy is lost between lovers than anywhere else. People use much of their energy to control their mate, to own each other's bodies, to make them see their point of view is all things and to get them to worship their body as God's gift to the human race. This is the consciousness that will bring about the spirit of death in the most healthiest of bodies and to the best of relationships. These games are not only wicked and sick, but they will surely be the death of the body.

One thing that all spirits understand is that control and possession is a BIG mistake. Yet, they do it all the time and pretend that they would never do anything like that to another human being. All that these spirits are really doing is not making these games conscious so that they can go on playing them until they are all played out. These games require a lot of life force energy to play effectively. Whatever way in which you want to be seen by your friends and lovers is where you will direct your energy to create that illusion. You may want to look prettier, healthier, richer, smarter or more spiritual than you really are. But the problem is that eventually, whoever it is that you are trying to fool will break through that veil of illusion and see you as you really are. (Which in reality, is probably much more beautiful than those silly illusions.) Between creating illusions for yourself and putting energy in someone else's head or genitals to control them, and getting them to do the things that "Make you happy", you are lucky to even get your body to function at all. That just shows you the abundance of energy that the Supreme Being has given to each of His children. With all of these energy games going on all of the time, people still manage to function each day.

At the same time all of these human love games are in play, the same spirit enforces some meaningless code of false ethics and morals on his/her own body. Most of these "ethics and morals" do not even belong to the spirit, let alone the body. Ethics and morals do not belong in the body at all. The body at best, must be harnessed, not suppressed. Harnessed in a way in which it will not give away or lose all of it's energy. Harnessed in a way in which it can learn how to regenerate itself, rather than a continual degeneration process that it was programmed for. Any suppression will stagnate the individual's energy, and as mentioned above, the lack of flow of energy is death to the body.

Dwelling in the personality is another cause of the body's death. When you are in the personality consciousness, all there is is death. In this state, you are not aware of yourself or anyone else as spirit. Death as you can see comes in many forms, such as hate, human love, addictions …etc. These are the result of non-awareness of spirit. The personality and body cannot see spiritual things without the spirit. The spirit must look through the body/personality, thereby including the body/personality in the life of the spirit. When the body looks around without the spirit consciously being in it, it can only see material things, and all material things are in a constant process of death or decay. As the body/personality looks upon this condition of "life" on earth, it sees that life is a constant process of dying and decaying, and, as we all should know by now: what you see is what you get.

All bodies, so far, are programmed for death. This death program creates a "death urge" that is so powerful that few in the history of man have been able to overcome it. Do not despair, for all human beings will eliminate this death urge in the New Age. But we here must do it for ourselves. This urge will subconsciously guide the body/personality to the grave. Step by step, from the time of about twenty-one years old the body begins to die and continues to die until you the spirit drops the body and finally lets it die, or until you just can't keep it alive any more. The urge in the body is to return to it's original essence. Can you blame it? By the time most bodies reach adulthood, they are totally abused and perverted on an energy level, on an emotional level and on a physical level. If you were a body, wouldn't you look forward to transition under these conditions? Because of this, many have a death wish - they wish to die. Really though they are transferring the bodies wish to die to themselves.

This is not always the case though. Many spirits long for death to alleviate the self-inflicted pain of knowing what they have done to their bodies and what they themselves have become. But this wish for death will not be satisfied. Spirits are truly immortal and must transmute all the darkness to find peace. For you reading this, please hear this: now is the time to transmute while you still have a physical body. It will become increasingly difficult as time goes on, especially if you lose that body. People on their deathbed are always fighting for one more breath. Regardless of how miserable they felt their life was here in the three-dimensional world, there must be something pretty special about being here, because people are always fighting to keep the body alive at that last moment.

During this time of transition, (transferring from the physical world to the spiritual world), one has the opportunity to review their life on this planet. The spirit then is "forced" to review all "wrong" conscious choices during life. When the body is shed, like an old coat, nothing seems to have changed for the spirit. The spirit moves into an emotional, or astral body, and enters a state where everything is as it was during life. Because of this, many spirits do not even know that their body has died. But soon, friends and relatives that have previously made the transition will begin to appear and greet them. At this time they have the opportunity to talk about anything or everything.

This state lasts for seventy-two hours. At the end of that time the spirit is directed to a level of the astral plane. This level is the level in which the spirit has evolved to during his/her life in the body. There are seven levels of the astral. The four lower levels are what some religions call "hell" or "purgatory". This is where most souls enter their spiritual life. Here, it is their task to give up all emotional games that they played while in physical form. And they must here give up all attachments to the physical world. In other words, they must learn neutrality. That is, they must learn neutrality if they want to advance to what is called heaven. The Supreme Being always keeps everyone in freedom, which means that one is allowed to be in any level of the astral that they want to be in. So the spirits in the four lower levels of the astral at this moment can continue the personality games that they have been playing for as long as they want. All those around them are surely playing the same games, so they all feel "right at home" unaware of where they really are.

If you drop the body tonight, where would you be on the astral planes? If you do not know, then you have much work to do! It is your job while in a physical body to clean out the four lower levels of the astral planes from your space. But do not panic, whatever you do not complete while in the body, you can do without the body. Understand

that it is much, much easier with the physical body than without it. If you do not believe me, then ask some of your "dead" relatives that are still stuck on the earth plane. If you do see this truth, then you will show it in your actions by becoming sincere about this Teaching and doing what is necessary to heal yourself of the "hell" within. You know in your heart of hearts what you are doing and what must be done. Are you doing it? As I often like to say: "Just do it!"

One of the principles of this Teaching is to make death your servant, rather than you be the servant to death. So in essence, death does not stalk you as it does mortal men and women, you capture death and use death for your own purposes. Let's say that you have a picture in your space that you do not need any longer. Then the practical thing to do is to purify that picture by turning it back into it's original essence. Our definition of death above is something returning to it's original essence. So by blowing pictures, and purifying your space, you are bringing death to a part of your body/personality, or as we say in the business, "dying unto self". Your body/personality dies daily unto you the spirit every time you run your energy, blow roses, ground, do psychic readings, and perform an Avatar Power ritual. You are purifying a part of yourself, turning it into golden white energy, which is what you are as a spirit. As your body/personality dies or submits to you the spirit, the death urge is relieved a little at a time. And soon the body/personality stops walking in the direction of death (darkness) and walks towards life (light). Thereby becoming more and more light as you walk with your body to The Light.

As you walk along the path of Life, you will clean out the body's addictions, programming and subconscious mind. As a matter of fact, in cleaning out the body's addictions, programming and subconscious mind, you are

Michael C. Fikaris

walking along the path of LIFE. These are one and the
same.

Chapter Thirteen

DIVINE LOVE

Most people do not understand what true love is. We have all been raised to have a false idea and image of love. Whether it is the love of a lover, mate, mother, father, brother, sister or friend, what we have been lead to understand as love is not real. I do not know when we lost our understanding of love, but I do know that it has happened a long, long time ago.

Now, most of you reading this are sitting there saying, "No, not me. I know what love is." Well, you don't, and I will not spend a lot of time proving this to you. Eventually, you will see the truth about what love is and what you think it is now, and you will see the difference. In the meantime, just look at your relationships with people. Do you feel truly loved? Who do you love unconditionally? Who loves you unconditionally?

To really know what love is, we must first deprogram what love is not. This can be done in many ways, if one pays attention to life's lessons and learns to let go. I'll give you a short cut right now: think about all of your ideas of what love is, look at all of the movies you have seen about love, remember all of the books you've read about love, take everything your parents taught you about love, and take everything that your lovers have taught you about love… now, gather all of that information and just go ahead and flush it down the toilet. Really, it should be burned up, but it would pollute the atmosphere and affect someone else nearby. At least flushing it will send it somewhere safe, away from other humans. Now, do not worry if you have accidentally learned something valuable about love from any of these people or experiences. Remember, "what is real cannot be threatened". If you actually know anything about love, you will know it forever. But the safest way to understand love is to start from the beginning and just assume that you know nothing.

This is usually as far as people will go. Most of you will stubbornly hang on to your old concepts and programming about love because you are afraid of change. Afraid of losing something. Fear of loss of love. What is funny is that people fear losing what they do not have! You have been given hate and death and told it was love. How did you know? Your whole life you were lied to by people who didn't know they were lying! Now, I am telling you that what you have invested a lifetime into is a false and terrifying reality. Even worse: the opposite of love - death. And if you continue living this way, you will surely die. Not exactly what people want to hear. But, this is the message that life is so persistently trying to give to you.

Spiritually speaking, the urge in the woman is to follow her man. (For most now days, this is a subconscious urge). This is easy if he is a true man of God, walking into the Light, or if he is going in the direction she wants him to. A woman must discern who her man really is, and if she wants to walk that particular path. When she adds her energy to his, their growth is quickened along the path. She gives the power which launches them both into the Light. This creates a divine need for one another: his direction and her power. Both are equally important. When a woman dominates a man, she will quickly loose respect for him and become bored with him. She cannot respect one that is so easily controlled. And because almost all women have little true self respect or self worth, then the man who worships her and bends to her will becomes even more of the fool.

Today's men are weak. One woman I know calls them nothing more than "trained monkeys". It is obvious why so many women have no respect for men, or even hate men.

When both are healed, strong and clear, there is no apparent leader or follower. Both lead and follow within a divine flow. It appears from time to time that one may be leading or dominating, but the truth is that they are really following the Universe together. In this reality, there is no competition, or even a thought between the two about leadership roles, dominance, or control. Both see and submit to the God nature in one another.

In the spiritual relationship, the woman romances her man. She initiates sex with him more of the time and creates most aspects of the relationship. This is a woman's domain and where her power exist: Love and sex. By doing this, the relationship will always be fun and exciting. She will be free to create her fantasies, and experience her desires.

Men have no business chasing women. They are incapable of knowing what a woman really wants, and he can only romance her for short periods of time, doing only the things that he has learned from past relationships or has read about. This is not really romance. Each woman is different and has her own ideas of love and sex.

A woman teaches a man how to make love to her. True, he can show her a few things, but that is not what I mean. It is more of an inner thing. At the same time, men have to learn when and how to say "no" to a woman. Most men will have intercourse a woman whenever she wants him. This is not good for either person. There are times when a woman wants sex for the wrong reasons. It is the man's responsibility to look clairvoyantly and ask "Is this good for her?" If the answer is no, then he must abstain, regardless of his own desires. And she must not become upset, but know that his actions are for her good.

97

Michael C. Fikaris

Sex should be a meditation at all times... a really FUN meditation. And it should be approached that way. The man must treat the woman as if she is the temple of God or the Church. Enter her with reverence and respect, not anger, or lust. And she must receive him as the Christ: open, receptive and pure in her love for him. This allows for the highest states to be achieved. No games: just a giving and receiving from a gold vibration.

Communication is very important, and this too is the woman's strength and the man's weakness. The woman needs to learn to communicate to the man when needed, rather than waiting for weeks, months or even years to say something. What usually happens is the woman ends up hating her man because of a build up of things that she never resolved with him. And he never really understands what is going on.

He needs to learn to hear his woman. Really tune into what she is saying, ask her questions until he is certain of her meaning, wants and needs. He also needs to be more colorful with his words, paint pictures for her rather than just one word answers all of the time. In other words, he needs to learn to talk *to* her rather than *at* her - communicate in a way she can hear what he is saying and meaning.

When a couple gets married, (usually, not in a divine love relationship, but the vast majority that marry), they both relax into a different mind set. She has reached her goal, so she changes gears. She slows down, and begins to nest. This is OK, except for what she sees in the mirror. She notices in time a drop in energy. She has lost her enthusiasm and love for her man. This is bad for both. Often, she stops working on herself and stops growing. She has reached a goal and that goal is not what she thought it would be. Her knight in shinning armor turned out to be just an everyday man after all. Soon, she begins to see the negatives in the man she married. She tries to change him - bring him to his true potential that she fell in love with, but she becomes frustrated because she can't. The more she tries the further away from that vision he drifts. Soon she looses interest in his life, and her sexual desire for him drops off... almost completely. She wants sex, but he does not inspire her anymore. This is the final blow. Every couple needs sex in order to maintain a valid relationship. In reality, women need sex more than men do.

While all of this is happening, the man is trying to impose his control over her. Often demanding that she does not change or submits to ridiculous demands or behavior. If she looses her individuality, then he will become bored with her and wonder what happened to that strong independent woman he fell in love with. On the other hand, if she fights him over meaningless things, he will spend as much time away from her as possible.

Eventually, she will become over dependent on him for too many things: her happiness, her social life, her emotional well being, money, courage,... etc. At some point, he can't keep up. She looses what is left of her self-respect. And all aspects of real communication stop, including sex. This is when she either dies on the inside or leaves him and starts a new life. Few women will leave their man. Usually, the woman will unconsciously arrange for him to leave her or to find another woman. Either way, she gets screwed emotionally because she will then see herself as a victim.

To avoid all of this, either do not get married, or pretend that you are still single, trying to catch the man you love, (even if you already have him). And, most importantly, communicate. Write to your man at least once per week telling him everything that is bothering you and everything that you love. It is mostly important to release the negative.

Michael C. Fikaris

Women tend to carry resentment for a long time and this poisons their system emotionally, mentally and sexually. Writing a weekly "love letter" enables the couple to resolve things on a regular basis and allows the man to know what is going on with his woman. Most men do not have a clue how women feel or see things. And, of course, as a woman, take power in the relationship. Create what you want and do not wait for him to do it. He may or may not, that is not the issue. The point is to go for what is important to you, otherwise you will probably be disappointed.

Men, you must learn to respond, not react. Pay attention and know the woman you are with. Most men do not know who they are married to. Be firm, yet gentle and loving. And above all, be giving in all ways. Do not stifle your woman or try to keep her in the same place mentally, emotionally or physically.

What is required of both men and women at this point is a leap of faith. Or at least a step in the right direction. Some will take a small step at a time towards true love. A very few will leap. Most will never change, yet think they have. At the very least, I hope that you read on and then try just one baby step.

Remember a time, if you can, when you were in love with someone new. A new lover, a new relationship. Feel how that was. Feel the enthusiasm and excitement you had during that first few weeks. The joy you felt. How maybe you felt you could do anything - no fear. Remember how healthy you were during that time. How little you needed to sleep or eat. How high your energy was. Feel that feeling right now... Try not to read on until you feel it...

What happened to that? Most people think that that is not really love, but something else that brings people together. The truth is, that is love. The problem is, most do not understand it. It happens unconsciously and by accident.

100

In the subconscious mind is the belief that it cannot last, therefore, it doesn't. The reality is that we were made to be in that same state of consciousness every single day of our lives. "Impossible" you say? No, not impossible at all. Natural is more like it. What you have not experienced or ever even seen is hard to believe. Maybe even hard to imagine. But so is most of what is real and heavenly. The Divine is something that is buried deep within your mind, long forgotten, but awaiting your awakening.

Love is a power; a force that can transmute and heal anything in our reality. Love is an idea, a feeling, a knowing of self, an understanding of Creation, and an un-limiting power. Love has no beginning and no ending. It is on going, regardless of any circumstance or experience, whether positive or negative. To experience Divine Love with another living soul, is to know the divinity in creation, it is to experience God. When you truly know someone, you know God within them. To know God is to know love. It is impossible to know God and not love. This is a step in knowing yourself.

But we were taught the ways of a lessor way of life. A life where illusions are accepted as reality. First and strongest is the belief in lack. Lack of money, lack of health, lack of food or substance, lack of friendship, lack of self worth, even a lack of love. The illusion of lack is the basis of all illusion. And the basis of *that* illusion is the illusion of lack of love.

When we are filled with divine love, (true love), no lack can exist on any level. Again, remember that feeling of true love, what was lacking in your life during those times? During those times, we experience only fulfillment on the deepest levels and even our true selves as spirits of light.

The fact is, that we cannot be in lack of love. This is because we ARE love. We, as spiritual beings, in essence

101

are love manifested in human form. Expressing ourselves as who we are is expressing love. When we are truly loving, we are being ourselves. We were created from love as the love of the Creator. It is the divine love from the Creator that ensures our existence. If for one moment we were not totally loved, we would cease to exist. It is our sustenance, our lifeblood.

Nor can we be limited in any way, except what we accept in our own minds. Our own lack thinking of ourselves is the only thing that can truly limit us in life. We are children of God - Sons and Daughters. We have everything within ourselves as does the Creator. Nothing was withheld on any level. As the Course of Miracles states many times, this reality can be realized in a Holy instant.

What causes this condition is the illusion of the "separation" and fear. One engenders the other. The illusion of the separation between us and the Creator has been programmed for thousands of years and reinforced continuously from the time of birth. All that is good or God is described as outside of ourselves. We wait for our good to happen, rather than creating our own good daily on a conscious level. We have been disempowered through a systematically programmed false identity.

Our misunderstanding of love has caused us to crave an inferior base substitute that will always force us to look for an outside fix. It is like a drug. People get addicted to drugs, alcohol… etc., because they like the way the drug makes them feel. They do not realize that they can get the same feeling naturally from within and that it would be a real feeling, so they continue to use the artificial substance for the effect. Well, false love is the same. People continue to look to other people to satisfy their inner urge for love. This will never work. True love only comes from within. Yes, we do crave a mate and family. But these things will never satisfy what is truly desired on an inner level.

Possessiveness, control, jealousy, manipulation, domination, fear, competition, suspicion, suppression, torture, judgment, criticism, complaints, worry, anger, sexual manipulation, sexual games and any form or mental, emotional or physical abuse are all aspects of this false love. This is what is taught to the world as love. None of these concepts exist in a Divine love relationship. Divine love is freedom, joy and life expressed on all levels at all times. It is a constant free giving from the heart.

In fact, to truly experience love, you must always be ready, able and willing to give totally and freely. Such a simple concept. Yet one that requires a leap of faith. It is a true act of love in the highest sense. It requires that on some level, you must except your Divinity. You must admit, at least intellectually, (the most basic level), that you are truly a Child of God, and as such, you can give freely of yourself, without fear whatsoever. You must be willing to give up your lack consciousness. You must accept the truth that you are an unlimited being and then act upon that realization in all ways. Gradually, you will transform yourself from a taker to a giver - your true Godlike nature. Little by little, as you learn to give, through the giving you will experience love. You will learn to love all of God's creations at all times. You will learn to love freely and unconditionally. Inspiring people to be free rather than trying to hang onto them. Through the process of continually giving and expressing love, you will receive indescribable feelings of love from the Universe welling up within you, enabling you to express love more at deeper levels. You will never be without love again and the illusion of the separation between you and the Creator will be non-existent in your consciousness forever.

103

Michael C. Fikaris

As you take this first step, you may experience conflict. Do not fear. Again, an act of faith is required here. The conflict is based on the misunderstanding of giving and having. Most do not see that through giving only, is having possible. People have been conditioned to believe that you must have an abundance in order to give. The opposite is true. To have an abundance, then you must learn to give an abundance. What is given to you depends upon your true desire and ability to give to others. If you want money, then give money; if you want love, then give love; if you want joy, then give joy. As you give to others, the Universe will give to you, so that you are more enabled to give more of the Creator's essence in many forms.

Soon your "having" turns into "being". Being a channel for the good of others. Being a representative of the Light. Being an incarnated aspect of the Creator. Being your true spiritual self.

What is within us, is what we will express, and through that expression, whether it is with words or actions, we will promote either war and conflict or Love and Peace. To teach is to learn. All teachers know that the best way to learn is to teach. As one is teaching, (giving information and understanding - or themselves standing under what is real and true), new information and understanding comes into them. To have Love and Peace, teach it, or in other words: give Love and Peace to others.

To succeed in this, you must clearly choose. You must choose to resolve the conflict of giving and of the separation. Thus bringing peace within yourself. You must decide clearly that you will live under the Divine system of the Universe and no longer participate in an illusionary and meaningless reality. This decision and your action following it, will be your step out of conflict. By teaching Love and Peace, giving what you know to others, you will demonstrate to others your true nature and then become who you are in reality.

Now you must embrace what you know. You must be consistent in all ways and in all aspects of your life. You must use your will power to consistently choose truth and reality over illusion. By resolving conflict in yourself, you now see clearly the illusions made my men, and you must reject the illusions of hate, war and conflict and embrace the Oneness of the Kingdom of God. This will elevate you to a higher level of being.

Now you will become the love of the Universe. And only love will flow through you. Your mind will be one with the mind of the Christ and the Holy Spirit, and your true Will will manifest in this dimension. Love will be your teaching tool, your healing balm and your power.

Throughout our past, we have built our experiences upon special relationships with other people. Good or bad, we continued with these relationships, regardless of how limiting they were. Fear and not truly understanding the Universe has kept us from moving forward in our evolution as a race of people; therefore, limiting our experiences with others. Thinking that we can only have one mother or one father, or only our children can be fathered or mothered by us, has put the human race into a box, limiting our expression of love. Why do people treat other people's children with less love than their own? Why can't people look to older and wiser individuals for guidance? Why must we withhold love and admiration from those of the opposite sex, unless we are married to them or have some special relationship with them? Why do we limit our love for people and life?

To move forward, you must erase your past. As I said in the beginning of this chapter, take everything you have learned about love and flush it down the toilet. See the ones you love as spiritual beings, not mothers, fathers, lovers or your children. See everyone as an aspect of God, a spiritual brother or sister. Remove the pastime labels. This will enable you to love more freely and unconditionally without prejudice or fear.

Think about the last time you committed a totally unselfish act of love. Remember that feeling for a moment. Recall how pure and wonderful it was. Remember the joy and excitement you felt during that time. Don't just read these words. Really do it! Bring back that feeling for just a moment... right now. What could be better? What can bring more to life than love in action? Commit random acts of kindness and love each and every day, and your life will always be filled with love and joy. You are the love and you must become the Way, the Truth and the Life. This is true freedom. And Divine love is freedom. "Teach only Love, for that is what you are."

Chapter Fourteen

MALE ENERGY

Male energy, female energy and the differences between the two are probably the most misunderstood concepts on the planet. The funny thing is that the true purpose of these differences are designed to compliment one another and to make life more meaningful, more enjoyable and much easier for everyone. Quite the opposite has happened. People are always saying that they do not understand the opposite sex. Men and women represent the duel nature of the Creator, so understanding the opposite sex is the same as understanding an aspect of God. The aspect that you do not carry fully within yourself. So, one nature is within us and the other nature is in front of us. As we mate with the other gender, the two become one and both natures come together as One - the Father/Mother God manifested. Because of this, all people have the urge to mate. Unfortunately, this urge has been perverted into acts of sex that are not only unnatural, but quite often degrading, and almost never the true spiritual experience it is meant to be. People's perspectives have become more animalistic, selfish and demented through time - especially in recent history.

The other gender for most people has become like an addictive drug: hated but very much craved. People often say, "Can't live with them and can't live without them". Now days, I've even heard people say "Can't live with them and can't kill them". This shows the attitudes between the sexes today. Women have been openly expressing their anger and resentment for men for quite some time now. And

107

blaming a man or men for most problems is an age-old way of life among the women of the world. Recently, men have begun to do the same things: blame, anger and resentment. The only way out of this dilemma is to take full responsibility for one's own life and to learn to love and appreciate the other gender for who they are. In the chapter entitled "Victimization of the Human Race" I discuss in detail responsibility. So, now the more difficult part of the solution: to love and appreciate.

What people do not realize is that the war between the sexes and not truly loving, understanding and appreciating each other does nothing more than keep all people weak. This consciousness keeps people in the dark about the Creator and the Universe. It distracts people from taking the necessary spiritual steps while on this planet. Many become so obsessed with trying to resolve relationships, understand the problem or just get what they want from their partner, that they cannot clearly see reality. They cannot invoke the God Nature within themselves because they do not understand their own God nature very well and they understand the other gender even less, if at all. So all of the good, the power and joy that mating is supposed to bring for both people only lasts for a short time, usually in the beginning of the relationship, then everything begins to decay and turn into a powerfully negative and destructive force.

So, how do we heal this on going pattern? Simple... Forgiveness. Forgiveness is essential in order to love and appreciate. But to forgive, there must be understanding. In understanding, one can then learn the appropriate lessons and information and then more easily let go of all resentment and hate.

For this chapter, I will write about male energy. With this, I hope to bring understanding for both men and women about men. I would like to write about female energy as well, but I will leave that to the much more qualified and incredible women on the planet. I do wholeheartedly recommend for both men and women a book called *A Woman's Worth*, by Marianne Williamson. It is truly a wonderful book about women!

I have a T-shirt with a picture of a man that reads: "Save the Males". When I wear this shirt I get no responses from men and many interesting responses from women: some positive, but mostly negative or sarcastic. Unfortunately, the truth is that the males do need saving. At this point in time, men are leaving the planet at a fast rate: there are over 100 wars, killing mostly men; AIDS, killing mostly men and designed to kill men; gang wars and drug related death, killing mostly men or boys; less percentage of boys are being born now then in any other time in history; the male sperm count has dropped 75% since the mid-1970's, men are becoming impotent, which spiritually translates to a loss of power and a loss of creative ability; plus men are dying of the usual heart problems and other diseases at increasing rates.

There are many reasons for this. First and foremost is that whoever does not make the transition into the New Age will not be allowed to stay on this planet. This transition requires many changes within, and men do not like to change. Any woman who has married a man thinking that she can change him, can attest to the fact that there are few things more difficult than trying to change a man. (Remember that ladies the next time you get involved with a man. Either love him the way he is or leave him alone). This nature of not wanting to change is a negative thing if you have taken on negative habits and perspectives. A high majority of the men on the planet today have. And because of the energy changes, these negatives cannot survive and neither will the men that express them.

If the man is already negative, unstable, inconsistent and undependable, then it is unlikely that he will change for the better. On the other hand, if his habits and perspectives are positive, then this nature brings stability, consistency and dependability. And because his nature is to not change, then these characteristics will become stronger as time goes on. These positive traits are the ones that should be natural to a man and these are some of the traits that a woman looks for in her man.

Unfortunately, now days, these positive attributes are not passed down from father to son anymore. Most boys that grew up in the fifties, sixties, seventies or eighties have not really had positive interactions with their fathers. Most fathers from those days to now were working constantly or separated from the family because of divorce. And if not, they were separated on an energy level because of their inability to communicate in a real and loving way. Consequently, the majority of the world's population today, both male and female, have not been fathered correctly. This has created several problems in today's society for both sexes. For men, this situation has created a lack of understanding of how to be a man. Many men have learned about manhood from their mothers, or quite often from movies or television. The problem here is obvious: none of these can teach a boy to be a man.

Being a man is not in the behavior. It is an energy, a vibration and a perspective. And this energy and perspective is much needed today. Boys should learn about male energy and perspective from experience with roll models. Usually from their fathers or possibly from older brothers. If neither exists, then they will learn from wherever possible, right or wrong. But the male vibration and perspective cannot be demonstrated by a woman or by an actor playing a roll. This just creates confusion.

Men, by nature are born to provide for others. It is a tragedy that today's society and economy has taken so many men out of their work. I see no problem whatsoever with women being in the workforce. The problem is in the men. A man needs to be productive in order to maintain his sense of self. A man that is not productive will die on the inside within a short time. It is his true nature to provide for those that he loves, or if he is single, then to begin to build for that future family. Unfortunately, today it has become common and acceptable for men to not work and to live unproductive lives, being taken care of by the government or a woman. Either of these situations is psychologically and spiritually devastating for an otherwise healthy man. Little by little he will deteriorate into negativity and destructiveness. Destroying not only himself, he will also eventually take down those around him. A man needs to be encouraged and supported in his chosen work. And most importantly, a man needs to choose to work at all times.

Some of the God aspects that men represent on this plant are focus, purification, understanding, simplification, direction and light .

Focus: We live in an age of distraction where people's attention is limited to about 15 seconds at a time. Focusing is a lost art for most people today, yet focus is necessary in order to manifest prosperity or the spiritual into the physical. Men, by nature, can only focus on one thing at a time. To focus on many things at once for a man is nonproductive. It scatters his energy. A man's focus is like a magnifying glass bringing the sun's rays into a single point or intensity. For a clear and positive man, this is a powerful tool. The tool that enhances or empowers his other positive attributes.

111

Michael C. Fikaris

Purification: This is his ability to eliminate from life or the planet what is no longer needed or valid. Men, when healed, can use this ability to cleanse the old or negative from within himself or the family structure. He can help to bring death to what is blocking the good of those around him - death (or purification) to fear, negativity, false concepts, interference or blocks of all kinds.

Understanding/Simplification: Understanding comes from the ability to simplify. Where women have the ability to expand, men can reduce. They can take something quite complicated and bring it to it's most basic essence and through this process, more clearly understand the nature of things at the core.

Light: This is probably the most subtle, but most important aspect of the male gender. At the purest level, men represent the Light of the Creator. This is what women mostly want from men in the deepest part of the subconscious mind. This Light represents the Christ consciousness. It is passed from the man to the women in many ways, but most directly during sex through his sperm. In that essence is his consciousness as a spiritual being, and if he is a spiritual man, then that sperm fills the woman with the Light of the Christ as it is absorbed into her bloodstream. The Light also becomes a guiding light, lighting the way along the path into a heavenly state of consciousness. This Light, coupled with the woman's Power, enables the two to accomplish any and all things on this planet for their and their family's highest good. (Interestingly, as mentioned before, the average male sperm count is down by 75%. This symbolizes also the lack of light or spiritual understanding.)

Being a spirit in a male body is not about being macho or acting in any particular way. It is about being focused, centered, and living with integrity and compassion. Women

112

are not looking for physical muscles, they are looking for spiritual muscles. Rather, men with inner strength and determination of Light.

Michael C. Fikaris

Chapter Fifteen

HEAL THY SELF

I have been studying healing now since 1981. Not a lifetime, although it seems like it. When I started my training in the early summer of 1981, the first formal class I took was basic healing. At the time, I wasn't consciously interested in healing, but it was the only class that I was willing to take in this particular institute. As it turned out, I received very good techniques and had many important experiences in that class, but not enough to really turn me on to healing. In those days, I was more of the intellectual type seeking information rather than practical spirituality. Later, through the years, I realized that healing comes in many ways, shapes and forms. There are probably as many ways to get or give a healing as there are people in the world. A healing can come through a smile, a look, a word, an action, an energy, a spirit, a drop of rain, a ray of sunlight, a thought, or a touch. A healing can come as a tincture, a tea, an herb or even a mushroom/garlic pizza... but only if it is Sicilian style. Teachers, clairvoyant readers, counselors, guides and therapist are all healers. So are lovers, friends, relatives and even enemies.

Healing comes in many ways, shapes and forms. Let's look at the condition of healing in the world today. Since 1993 I have been guided to take a much closer look at the healing processes that takes place. Today the medical profession is moving at a snail's pace towards the truth about healing. What the spiritual Masters have taught for thousands of years will be eventually scientifically proven. But in the meantime, we must put up with half-truths and total lies coming from a money motivated, control oriented profession. Many doctors have made remarkable discoveries, but their hands are tied in many ways. True healers are rare in the medical profession and they are constantly challenged in the US by the Food and Drug Administration and the American Medical Association. This is the situation not exists in the US, but throughout the world. Even countries with socialized medicine have to deal with the greed of the chemical and medical supply companies.

In the last century or so, especially the last 50 years, a tragedy of great proportions has taken place in the world. People have given up their authority in every conceivable way. Not only in their living conditions, financial conditions and personal freedoms, but also in their own personal health. The knowledge of "healthy mind, healthy body" is now regarded as some archaic myth rather the reality that it is. Today, as incredible as it sounds, people actually believe that a doctor can heal them! The funny thing is (or sad thing I should say), is that even the doctors know that they cannot heal anyone. Yet this lie persists and it is continually reinforced by their silence. Never will you hear a doctor tell you that you can heal yourself or that it is your own mind and belief that will heal your problem. Yet, they have known this fact for quite some time now. For obvious reasons, they prefer a system of dependency. This keeps them in business and keeps the population sick.

The difficult thing is to convince people that they have been fooled, or really conned into the whole medical trap. It is system based upon hopelessness, helplessness and victimism rather than faith, self-reliance and power. But even with the knowledge that the public does have, the programming and fear runs so deep that 99% of the population will not take the necessary steps to good health and well being. Let's look at it logically: 1. The "placebo effect", (healing people with sugar pills), has been known by all people in the developed countries for decades now. Did this change people's attitudes about medication? No! 2. It is known by science that the human body can create any chemical known to man and it does upon command or belief. Did this change people's attitudes about medication? No! 3. Some people are healed by a medication and others are not, although given the same dosages under the same conditions. Did this change people's attitudes about medication? No! People still believe in the power of the pill and the one who has prescribed it, rather than looking within. Looking at numbers 1-3 above, it is obvious that there is something illogical going on in the world. I had a Teacher once who said, "If you are going to take a pill, then at least say "I now give you the power to heal me!", because that is what you are doing anyway. At least this way you can increase the power of the pill!". A wise Teacher indeed. That was the last day I took a pill. That was the spring of 1982. Within 2 years I healed my allergies without doctors or pills.

The true problem is the money. There is no money in true healing. People are not supposed to get sick. And if they do, they are supposed to heal themselves. Once the person is truly healed, that's it. Period. End of story. They never get sick again. But what about the money? The trillions and trillions of dollars that goes into hospitals, doctors, treatments, drugs, equipment, research, insurance, etc.?! There are doctors in the world that today are healing cancer, AIDS, and many other "incurable" diseases, very quickly, simply and cheaply. Where are they? Usually in some third world country where they can practice true healing without being put in jail. It is amazing, we have flower remedies, herbal solutions, thousands of drugs for sale everywhere that are supposed to cure all kinds of things, but don't; yet, if someone says "I have the cure for cancer", and they really do, they go to jail. There are proven methods of healing cancer and AIDS within weeks for less than $200 total! Why doesn't the public know?! Simple: the average cancer patient spends $80,000 before he finally dies. (AIDS patients spend about the same). And this is after 50 years of research to find the cure for cancer!

I called the American Cancer Society in early 1996. The doctor I talked to told me that they really do not know very much about cancer. All they know is that it is growing rapidly throughout the world. One in eight women today will get breast cancer. That is 12% of the female population and that is only one form of cancer. What if you add all the other types for both male and female? One study from Sweden says 25% of the population has cancer in 1996. 25%!! When I look at this on a spirit level, I see at least 50% by the year 2002 will have a terminal disease - probably a form of cancer or AIDS. I know this sounds unbelievable. The truth is that people do not want to believe such things, so they don't. They won't even look. But whether I am right or wrong about the future is meaningless at this point. What is important is now, and how to heal yourself.

The tragedy of the whole medical system is beyond description. Even the most basic things they have told us are contrary to good health. Eating "three balanced meals per day" for example, is one of the worse things a person can do to the body. Vaccines: the whole vaccination system completely changes the body's programming for healing itself. Think about it: you are introducing viruses into the body! How can this strengthen the body? It is insane to think that that is a good thing, yet no one questions it because people believe everything that they are told by the "system". Vaccines disable the body's natural healing ability. When I realized this, I stopped giving shots to my children. My wife and I have twelve children and only two have had the normal shots. The other ten have had none. The two that have had their shots are constantly sick (about once per month which is the national average in the US for children. That statistic in itself is incredible!). The other ten children may get a cold once a year at the most and it will only last 2 days maximum. In addition, these other ten have never been to a doctor for anything at all. They naturally know how to heal themselves and it is not in their consciousness or in their belief that they need anyone outside themselves for healing.

Hermes, the Greek philosopher had a lot to say about healing. The most basic thing that he says about healing is that "Healing is a positive change of Vibration". An interesting way to look at healing: "A positive change of vibration". Most people would not even know what this means, let alone put this valuable information to good use. The truth is that everything vibrates. Even a rock. Understand that this is a basic law of nature. Today, it is common knowledge that what Hermes presented as a principle thousands of years ago has now been scientifically proven.

As a child, my mother would take me to the doctor all of the time. Because my older brother died suddenly, she feared that the same would happen to me, so I was carefully watched. During that time, I noticed that every time I saw a doctor it involved pain or discomfort - for me, not him. Eventually, I developed what I call a healthy fear of doctors. I call this a "healthy fear" because the fear kept me away from doctors for many years and consequently I have always been healthy. During my last visit to a doctor (the autumn of 1967), I decided that I would never see another.

118

After that day, whenever I was "sick", I would pretend that I was well and go about my daily routines: go to school, play sports, work, etc. This way my mother wouldn't know and I wouldn't have to see a doctor. What I discovered was that by the end of the day, I was healed. Isn't that interesting? I didn't understand how or why this happened until I started my spiritual training. As an adult, whenever I was "sick", I found that if I worked extra hard, rather than staying home and "being sick", then I would heal even faster. The answer to this is in the Hermes quotation above, "A positive change of vibration". I went from a "sick" vibration to a well vibration by acting well. This action created the opposite energy or "a positive change in vibration". This is the same philosophy I use with my children. If they have a cold or flu, then we do not make them stay in bed and "be sick". We allow them to do the normal things. This helps them to think they are well rather than sick, which enables the healing to manifest more quickly.

There is a famous story of the man who was quickly dying of cancer. He decided that he would spend his last days doing only his favorite things. His favorite thing was to watch Laurel and Hardy movies. So he bought all of them and then watched them over and over again. To the surprise of everyone, especially his doctor, he never died. Actually, he was completely healed within a few months, which was longer than he was supposed to live. "A positive change of vibration".

Neurolinguistic Programming demonstrates this truth quite well. If you are depressed, then rather than walking around and acting depressed, walk around with your head up, a smile on your face and act happy. And what you will find is that the depression will quickly pass. Of course if

119

you mope around with your head down, then it will last indefinitely. Again, consciously changing the vibration.

It is also known that many people get sick during or following bouts of depression. What has been more recently discovered is that the vibration of the person directly effects the individual's health - not only mentally and emotionally, but physically as well. According to the vibration of the body, certain chemicals are created within the body and then dispersed throughout. A low or negative vibration will create chemicals in the body that act as a poison and will make the body more susceptible to disease. A high or positive vibration will create antibodies and strengthen the body's immune system and increase resistance to disease. How does this work in a practical way? To know this, one must realize the true nature of the existence.

Dr. Deepok Chopra states that if you ask a physicist what the human body is made of, he will say 99% "air" or empty space. Of course, this is looking on an atomic level. The physical body is not a solid thing as is so widely believed. In reality, we are energy. More specifically, we are consciousness and our bodies are thought forms. This explains why some people are healed by certain medication and others are not. It is all about the mind and what the person believes will heal or not heal. In reality, the body is mind and must be treated as such for the healing to take place. Hermes states, "Man/woman is living mind, sustained by spirit. Mind (body) may be transmuted from state to state; degree to degree; condition to condition; pole to pole; vibration to vibration. Healing is the art and/or science of positively effecting a transformation of mind." True Hermetic transmutation or healing is a mental art. Healthy mind, healthy body. Simple truth.

A Time magazine article titled "Faith & Healing", June 24,1996, was dedicated to healing. This in-depth study revealed a little of the truth we are speaking of here. In the article, Time concludes that spirituality does help people heal and stay healthy. Time says the following, "According to a 1995 study at Dartmouth, one of the strongest predictors of SURVIVAL after open-heart surgery is the degree to which patients say they draw strength and comfort from religion... People who regularly attend religious services have been found to have lower blood pressure, less heart disease, lower rates of depression and generally BETTER HEALTH than those who don't attend". Regardless of your religious or spiritual beliefs, it is obvious that spirit or the mind is at work here. The doctors that do not believe in spirit must give credit to the mind, those that believe give credit to the spirit. Nowhere in the article did the doctor get the credit for these things related to religion or the mind.

Later in the article, Time examines the benefits of meditation. There is too much to quote here, so I recommend that you read the article, but I will give you one more: "Even skeptics such as Jarvis believe meditation and prayer are part of "good patient management". But he worries, as do many doctors, that patients may become "so convinced of the power of mind over body, that they may decide to rely on that, instead of the hard things, like chemotherapy". Let's hope that their fears come true, for that is the only path to true heath. We must rely on our own minds and spiritual nature if we truly want health.

To truly heal, we must learn to look at and treat the whole human being. To heal, we must realize that all of the parts are interconnected. That not only means different parts of the physical body, but also all aspects of the human being: spiritual, mental, emotional, as well as physical. So let's begin with the spiritual and work are way to the physical.

121

Michael C. Fikaris

SPIRITUALLY

Spiritually speaking, we must understand that whatever happens in this life on earth is designed to enable us to learn. Our primary purpose for being here is to discover who we are as spiritual beings and learn the necessary lessons that will enable us to become our true selves. With that in mind, we incarnate into a life that will bring to us the necessary situations, circumstances and opportunities for learning. In the process of learning, many things happen that people tend to perceive as negative or even tragic. This is the illusion of the world. The reality is that all experiences contain a treasure chest of knowledge. And the harder or more apparently negative the experience, the more treasure lies within it. But people today have been programmed to judge things as good or bad according to their preconceived ideas. So when the opportunity for learning presents itself, it is seen as a violation, punishment, bad luck, evil forces, karma or an accident. If one is limited by such perspectives then it is not likely to see the good in the experience and consequently miss the learning lesson. One must be open to receiving the good for it to be realized. If the person can only see negative, than that is all there will be. But the nature of the Universe is to give many opportunities to learn the same necessary lessons - so the lesson is repeated again and again in similar forms, each time increasing in intensity so that it will not be missed. For all people, a disease is a last ditch effort to learn what is probably a very simple lesson of life.

Realize that if you have contracted a disease, then you are not a victim. As a spirit you have a strong desire to learn in any necessary way. As a spirit you know that this world

122

is only an illusionary world designed for learning and that everything that happens here is by agreement. No exceptions… ever. (Read the chapter on Victimism). If consciously you are not getting the message, then the message will get stronger until you do. People that contract "fatal" diseases have one or more of these things in common: 1. A strong belief in victimism; 2. Resentment and emotional pain; 3. Unwillingness to change and grow; and 4. A negative perspective which creates negative habits such as negative thinking and speaking. All of these common traits are caused by not understanding life as it is and consequently, not taking responsibility for their own life.

Plus there is one more: Spiritual teachers have known for thousands of years that there are always many spirits around us. Some good spirits of the light, given to us to help us in times of need and to guide us through life. These spirits we call Angels of Light. In addition, there can be spirits of darkness around us. These are spirits that are negative in nature and they often can interfere with our spiritual path or make our lives more difficult. These spirits are sometimes called demons. It has been known for thousands of years that negative or dark spirits are part of the cause of disease, mental or physical. There are many spiritual practices which deal with disease on a spiritual level by removing these spirits from the suffering person. The most known example of this was Jesus. Throughout the New Testament are stories of Jesus "casting out demons" or "unclean spirits" and then instant healing or "miracles" would occur. He even directed His disciples to go out and to heal, teach and cast out demons.

What we see with people with disease or addiction, is another entity or spirit connected to the problem. Everything on this planet must be supported by a spirit.

123

Michael C. Fikaris

Every tree, plant, mineral, animal, human, virus or bacteria must have a life support system. All physical life is dependent upon the spiritual realms for it's existence. So a virus or a cancer cannot just exist on its own, it must be supported by a spiritual being. All of the cells in your body are kept alive by you. You are the support system for your cells. But who supports a virus or a cancer that is not compatible with your other cells? Can you support something that is not part of you and is in conflict with your body? That would require a duel nature within your inner most being, a nature that would fight against itself. And that couldn't be. You are who you are. But another spirit can give life to a virus, an addiction, or a bacteria.

How this happens is very simple and really quite obvious once you understand the process. There are always spirits around us. The type of spirits we attract depends upon the quality of our vibration and the lessons we need to learn. The lessons do not necessarily have to involve disease, but for many, who do not pay attention, this is the result. If you are expressing a positive vibration, thinking good thoughts and saying positive things, then you will attract angels of Light around you. If you are expressing negative vibrations, then you will attract negative spirits around you. This is the key. Like attracts like. A spirit cannot engage unless the vibration warrants it. A negative spirit or a spirit that supports a virus or disease cannot connect to the human body unless the body matches that particular vibration. To heal, one must not only drive away these entities, but also change the vibration within so to no longer attract them. An interfering entity has no power over anyone. They must be invited in by negativity or incorrect spiritual practices.

As a spirit in a body, you must take full responsibility for your life. This will empower you to heal and to thrive in all aspects of life. Until you take responsibility, then you are powerless to make a change - a positive change of vibration. If you believe that something outside of you has made you sick, then that thing has power over your life. But if you take responsibility and know that you created this situation, then you have the power to uncreate it or to change it for the better.

Step number one in healing: Ask within, "What do I need to learn from this experience? What is my lesson here? What is the Universe teaching me now? What spiritual information am I missing?" If you sincerely want to learn, then the answer will come. As it says in the Bible, "Ask and it will be answered". But you must be willing to hear the truth, because you may not like what you hear. If you are the type of person that cannot admit the mistakes that you've made then you will have trouble with this. Again, you must take responsibility. Blame or denial just will make your condition worse! It is foolish to die just to prove that you are a victim or that the illusionary world is real. In other words, do not choose death to prove your weaknesses are real!

After you have received your answer, you must then ask what to do. First the knowledge comes, then the knowledge must be put into action. Whatever comes, if you want to heal, then you must act accordingly without hesitation. This will change your vibration or effect a healing. Once the lesson is learned, there is no need for the pain or disease.

MENTALLY

Continuously we are bombarded with negative programming about our health. Every year in the fall, the advertising begins with statements of "fact" that it is now flu and cold season. Get ready because you are going to be sick now and when you get sick, here is what you need…

125

Michael C. Fikaris

This is the oldest sales trick in the book: create the need and then fill it. If the subconscious mind hears anything over and over again it will eventually believe it. Just try it sometime. Repeat something over and over again to someone or yourself and watch how it becomes a reality. My question is why should people get sick in the fall? Did the Creator create a time of year for everyone to get sick on purpose? Or did He just make another mistake? Or maybe the medicine companies realized that because the weather is cooling down that people would be more easily convinced that they are more susceptible at that time to sickness. The best one yet is the warnings on the cigarette packages. Every time now someone lights up a cigarette, the subconscious mind reads that warning, given by the Surgeon General - THE health authority! The end result? A few less smokers... maybe, a lot more cancer... for sure.

This is where we create our reality. Everything in your world comes from the mind. Again, Hermes states, "Man/woman is living mind, sustained by spirit." Change your mind, change your life. This takes work though for most people. The individual must go within the mind and see what is there. Within the subconscious mind are hidden beliefs, fears and an ocean of programming that is creating every aspect of life. These must be purged in order to manifest the changes in this dimension. The reason is obvious: Let's say for example that everyone in your family has died of colon cancer. Then subconsciously, there is an expectation that you too will die of colon cancer. Even if you consciously deny this, it will still lurk deep within the subconscious as a reality until it is removed permanently. Once this is done, then it will be healed. There must be agreement between the conscious, subconscious and super conscious minds. The subconscious is the most difficult to access, and it holds almost all of the programming. Once the

126

subconscious mind accepts the healing it will manifest in the body.

Who is the healer then? The mind. Even if it seems that the healing is coming from outside of the person, it is the mind that either accepts or rejects the healing. Remember as stated above, the body is a thought form or really just an extension of the mind: treat the mind and heal the body.

Step two: heal the mind. Remove all negative programming and beliefs within the mind. Eliminate all negative mental habits: negative thinking; negative expectations; criticism; complaining; victim perspective; lack of faith; lack of trust; fear; belief in illusion; and negative fantasy. Meditation is the key to accomplishing this. Even Time magazine and the doctors interviewed had to admit to the benefits and power of meditation. Through meditation (preferably an in the body, active system), one can make the subconscious mind conscious and transmute all negative (darkness) into positive (Light). This is called "mental alchemy". As you take out the negative you then can replace those things with the positive or the life you want to create. The mind is your workshop. What you create there will manifest here in this dimension. If you already know how to meditate, then you should be doing it DAILY. It has always been odd to me that people will bathe daily but neglect to clean their energy field and their mental body. As if the physical body was more important or something... The reality is that the condition of the physical body is totally dependent upon the condition of the mental body. Only through meditation will the body and mind become strong and healthy.

EMOTIONAL

Michael C. Fikaris

Dr. Richard Anderson (USA) states that it is now known that all diseases are related to the emotions. Does that mean that if one heals their emotions then the body will be healed? Well, yes and no. The emotional is, on many levels, tied into the mind. When you heal the mind, the emotions will follow. If you experience negative emotions, then there is a problem in perspective which comes from the mind. Negative perspective creates negative thinking which creates negative emotions and any of these create poison, toxic chemicals and disease in the physical body.

People today have been conditioned to be emotional. They haven't been taught to harness and use emotions correctly in a powerful way, therefore, their emotions use them. In other words, people are controlled by their negative or even positive emotions. And they do not know how to stop or transmute the emotion, thereby being helpless to come out of that particular state until it has run it's course. For some people that could mean weeks of depression or fear for no good reason. The basis of these emotions are again unconscious ideas, beliefs and programming. It is said that you are never upset for the reason you think. This is true. Virtually every emotional problem or reaction can be traced to some childhood experience or programmed belief.

True power comes through neutrality. This does not mean that the individual is like a robot or a zombie with no personality. Actually it is quite the opposite. When neutrality is achieved, then the person has all of the emotions available as powerful tools of expression. The only difference is that he or she does not fall victim to the emotion and uses it for good or healing purposes. And more importantly, it allows the person to keep their vibration at a higher level, which promotes health and healing.

128

Step three: harness and heal the emotions. Whenever you feel a negative emotion begin, rather than react emotionally, go inward and ask yourself "Why does this upset me?" When you get the answer, ask again "Why does that upset me?" And then do the same with every answer that you receive until you get to the basic core picture - the cause of this emotion. Virtually every time you will find the answer in a childhood experience. Example: Let's say you are driving along and someone next to you calls you an "idiot". Now logically, you shouldn't really care because you don't know this person and you will probably never see him again, but you are upset. So, rather than giving him the finger out the window, you hold it in and ask "Why am I upset? Because he called you an idiot. Why does that upset me? Because it is not true. So. Why does that upset me? Because you are being misjudged. Why does that upset me? It seems to happen a lot. When was the first time it happened? When your mother blamed you for starting fights with your little brother when you really didn't. What was I trying to learn as a spirit in this experience? To know who you are and it doesn't matter what other people think of you." Bingo! Now you must neutralize all these types of experiences in your life. Forgive everyone who has ever misjudged you and thank them for helping to teach you this all important lesson. Once this is done, you have gotten the healing and that emotion will not return, nor will those type of experiences.

When you can accomplish this with all emotions, then learning and life will become much more enjoyable and you will respond correctly and effectively to situations rather than react emotionally. And there will be a lot less wear and tear on you physical body.

PHYSICAL

Michael C. Fikaris

The Earth is a reflection of what we are doing to ourselves. Each of us is a cell of planet Earth. We are interconnected to her in ways that few understand. Because of this, is it important to know that what we do to ourselves affects the planet and what we do to the planet effects us personally. The pollution in the environment is a direct result of the pollution within the bodies and minds of the vast majority of the human race. As mentioned before, at least 25% of the population today is dying of cancer. Many do not even know it. I mention cancer not so much that it is reaching epidemic proportions, but because it is the result of society's mass consciousness today. It is the inevitable outcome of society's actions in their personal lives and in the world. What has been discovered as the causes of this and all other diseases validates what spiritual teachers have been teaching since the days before Jesus. Even Jesus taught how to remain healthy in the physical body, but this information was carefully removed from the Bible and stored away in basement libraries of the Vatican. Recently, certain doctors and researchers have made amazing discoveries that correspond to the old wisdom taught thousands of years ago. Most of this section will be information obtained through medical research.

I will begin with the work done by Dr. Richard Anderson: For the body to be healthy, there has to be a certain chemical and mineral balance. There are many factors that create or destroy these balances. The most important balance is the Acid, Alkalinity and pH. Alkaline minerals create in the body an alkaline system. When the system is alkaline, it allows the body to release toxins, poisons and all other types of pollution. In addition, alkaline builds the immune system, which prevent disease. It is very difficult to be over alkaline. The only way one can become over alkaline is to be first over acid.

Too much acid in the system causes many problems. It restricts the body from eliminating the toxins, poison and other pollution's that the body picks up. It destroys the immune system, and allows disease to manifest in the body. Plus it interferes with digestion, which causes many problems.

Acid is formed in the body in many ways. Emotions create more acid than anything else. Negative thinking also creates acid in the body and the wrong foods (acid foods) will create acid. At least 50% of the population today are over acid and 70% of the vegetarians. Every sick person has too much acid.

The pH (potential Hydrogen), balance of the body is very delicate. The blood should be 7.3-7.4. When your pH drops to 7.1, then you are sick. If it drops to 7.0, then you die. The cells should 7.2. The pH levels are controlled by breathing and alkaline minerals. Most people today are shallow breathers. This is caused by negative thinking. And most people today do not get the alkaline minerals that they really need.

As the alkalinity drops the acidity increases. This sets off a series of events that cause a multitude of problems in the body. One of the main things is sodium is lost. Because of the acid foods that people eat, the stomach cannot create the sodium bicarbonate needed for digestion purposes. When this happens, the smooch will take sodium from other organs in order to digest the food. This weakens the other organs and creates acidity in those organs. Any one who craves salt is someone that is lacking sodium. The problem is that the sodium in table salt does absolutely nothing good for the body. All it does is calcifies the bowls.

Michael C. Fikaris

The following is a brief explanation of what happens to most people to one degree or another according to Dr. Richard Anderson:

Process:

1. Too much acid

2. Stomach secretes sodium bicarbonate and takes from other organs - liver and kidneys. This is necessary to digest foods.

3. If liver gets depleted, bile becomes too acid - creates liver stones, interferes with liver's ability to cleanse and detoxify. If liver is deficient in sodium it will take sodium from stomach lining and joints. Creates stomach problems in digesting, ulcers, etc. & arthritis in the joints.

4. If Chime (food + stomach acid + bile) is too acid then mucus forms in intestines.

5. Then this turns to mucoid limiting the ability to absorb minerals through the intestines. This causes people to eat huge amounts of food, which makes the whole system work harder which magnifies the original problem of too much acid.

6. If kidney becomes too acid then it shuts down and becomes ammonia & creates kidney stones

7. Hinders digestion - creates fermentation which creates more acid. Undigested food is toxic. All

meats and cheeses take 72 hours to digest. During this time they ferment.

8. Starvation is cause of death in cancer - cancer cells feed on fermentation (so do parasites). Cancer patients have excessive protein in blood. Protein is acid forming (hard to break down and always ferments in body)

9. Most people now days eventually die of liver failure from toxins or some liver related disease. Toxicity is main cause of disease.

On a deeper level, there have been some very interesting discoveries. Some time ago (in the late 1800's), Dr. Louis Pasteur developed a theory that diseases are caused by germs and viruses from outside of the body. This is something that is contrary to spiritual truth. Spiritually speaking, we know that all people create their own reality, including disease. Immediately, the medical profession and chemical companies embraced this theory. Years later, Just before his death Pasture stated that he was wrong and that it is not the germs but the environment within the body that allows disease to manifest. But for the last 100 or more years, people have accepted the germ theory as truth without question.

The following is a quote from Dr. Richard Anderson:

Proof the germ theory is inaccurate:

1. It is common to find pathogenic bacteria in a healthy person with no disease, such as: diphtheria, pneumonia and tuberculosis.

2. It is common to find the disease without the bacteria

3. It often happens that when a disease organism is injected into an animal, the animal acquires a disease bearing no clinical resemblance to the original organism. Why? Because it's internal environment completely changed the original microbe.

4. After exposure, one person has a disease and another person doesn't. For example a classroom full of children all exposed to the same virus - not all will contract the disease.

Another scientifically proven truth is that every time we take a breath, we breath in every disease on the planet. Why then do we not contract all or even some of these diseases? Three reasons: 1. We must be at the vibration of a disease in order to contract it. It was recently proven the people do not even catch colds from one another. But what does happen is if the person matches the vibration of the one that is "sick", then that will allow the cold to manifest. But it has nothing to do with the spread of germs. 2. The correct environment must exist in order for germs to survive. 3. Within all bodies are an organism called somatids. Dr. Be'Champ, an associate of Pasture, discovered a living organism called Microzyma - now called "Somatid". In 1916 Dr. Enderlein found them as well. In 1985, just before his death, Dr. Enderlein was honored for his research of somatids, although he was ridiculed and attacked most of his life for his findings. Here is what he discovered:

1. They are found in the blood and cells of our bodies

2. Can't be killed in any way.

3. They are absolutely necessary for life.

4. They evolve and mutate into germs or even viruses.

5. They become parasitic, feeding on the garbage in our bodies, and can develop into organisms such as cancer cells.

6. By cleaning up the environment, then the parasitic mutants will disappear, much like flies disappear when the garbage is removed.

Doctors Pasteur, Be'Champ and Enderlein supported the toxicity theory which state that what we do to ourselves creates the environment for disease and germs to live. This is contrary to the germ theory that says we are not responsible for disease. One promotes self-responsibility (able to respond) and empowerment, the other promotes victimism, helplessness and weakness.

Another amazing discovery: In 1993 Dr. Hulda Clark (Canada), discovered an interesting thing. She had been doing cancer research for many years and suddenly one week found that all of her cancer patients had something in common: all of them had parasites (worms) in the liver. So she instantly began testing everyone she could who had cancer and found the same thing in all cases: parasites at the live, regardless of the type of cancer. Then she started testing AIDS patients as well and also found the same, plus parasites at the thymus gland (which regulates the immune system). This discovery lead her to study the parasites and the effect they have on the human body. In her research, she found that parasites in any part of the body other than the intestines is extremely damaging and eventually fatal. Even in the intestines, where they are most commonly found, they cause problems such as over eating, fat buildup, tiredness and digestion problems. But in other parts of the body, such as the liver, pancreas or heart, things become drastically worse.

The most common parasite she found was the Intestinal Fluke. This is a parasite that normally lives in the intestines of humans from time to time for a short period and then is flushed out through the bowls. While this parasite is in the intestines it will lay eggs. The eggs are then absorbed into the blood stream and eventually they are filtered out by the liver through the bowls. The eggs of the fluke normally would not hatch in the human body because they have a tough skin around them. Normally, the eggs end up in a stream or grass. This is because the fluke's natural habitat is in livestock, such as cows, pigs, chickens, goats, turkey, and so on. When these animals eliminate, the eggs go into the grass or streams where they attach eventually themselves to snails or slugs. There is a chemical within snails and slugs that breaks down the hard covering of the eggs and hatches them. Then the fluke goes through five stages of development and eventually is eaten by the animals eating the grass or drinking the water in the same area they began as eggs. The eggs are picked up by humans by eating these animals.

The problem is that the eggs now are hatching in the bodies. The reason this is happening is because of the chemicals that are accumulating at the liver. The liver filters most toxins and chemical out through the bowls, but because the bowls of most people are so clogged up now days, it is very difficult for the liver to flush everything out.

This creates a build up at the liver. In addition, there are certain chemicals that the liver cannot process. The main one is called Isopropyl Alcohol. Isopropyl and any derivative of it is used excessively throughout the world for many, many products. This is because it is so inexpensive and it is a powerful sterilizing agent. Coincidentally, this substance hatches the eggs of the fluke... at the liver. What Dr. Clark has discovered is as they go through their stages of development, they secrete chemicals that cause rapid growth of cancer cells. Soon the flukes are living and multiplying in the liver and of course feeding upon the liver. The good news is that the liver can regenerate itself and it can still function even with only 20% operating ability. The bad news is that liver problems are extremely hard to detect, and as the flukes multiply, so do the cancer cells. Eventually, these cancer cells will spread through out the body, finding the weakest area to attack, prostate, breast, colon, etc.

It is my theory that these cancer cells originate from somatids. They mutate into parasitic cells that are really designed to eliminate or eat up the toxins, the parasites and their excretions in the body. But because the body is so toxic and filled with poisons, they continue to spread to other contaminated toxic organs. But that is just my theory... let's go back to what is already proven.

What Dr. Clark has found is that not only is cancer and HIV caused by parasites in the body, but almost ALL diseases. (I say "almost" because she hasn't researched every one yet). And that once the parasites are removed, and the toxins and isopropyl are eliminated from the system, then the disease stops. Within weeks, people are completely healed of cancer, AIDS or whatever disease they have been struggling with.

Michael C. Fikaris

If you have a disease, then the first thing to do is to eliminate the parasites from the body. The average person has at least 10 different parasites feeding on their body and there are 140 possible types. You will eliminate 2 pounds of parasites if you are healthy, more if not. Only use herbal remedies for this. (Details will be listed below). Within six days to twenty-one days you will be parasite free.

The next step is cleanse and heal the system. To effectively treat the liver, one must treat the bowls as well, because the liver is dependent upon the bowls to eliminate toxic waste. We work on the bowels and liver to help the immune system by cleansing. This is the greatest immune booster known to science. If the immune system is strong that the body will heal at once. When the intestines and bowls are clean then the system begins to eliminate all toxins quickly. To effectively cleanse the system, there are specific herbs and a specific diet. This process takes approximately 5 weeks and is very easy and powerful.

As you are cleansing, you must eliminate all input of toxins and most importantly anything with Isopropyl. Once you stop putting in the isopropyl the liver will be able to eliminate the build up. But for this to happen, you must completely stop taking it in. You will be amazed at all of the products that contain isopropyl. The reason so many do is the cheap sterilization factor. So there are traces of it everywhere in our daily lives. It will be hard to let go of some of these products, but it is necessary for good health. I have done most of it naturally over the years and I don't miss a thing. It does not take long to adjust.

Products with Isopropyl or Benzene (DO NOT USE)

1. All shampoos, conditioners, hair spray

2. Deodorants, body creams and lotions

3. Perfumes, after shaves, colognes, oils, makeup

4. Shaving creams (Benzene-helps promote HIV/AIDS)

5. All soaps, detergents, cleansers

6. All toothpaste and mouth washes

7. Condoms (Benzene)

8. All processed foods

9. All canned foods, bottled drinks, bottled water

10. All coffees and most teas

Acid Causing foods: (DO NOT EAT)

1. All beef, pork, deer or any other meat product - parasitic

2. All poultry and eggs - parasitic

3. All seafood - parasitic

4. All dairy products - parasitic

5. Most wheat and grains

6. All processed foods

139

7. All fried foods

8. All distilled substances, except water (vinegar, alcohol, …etc.)

9. Most oils

10. All fermented products (tofu, vinegar, wine… etc.)

11. All spices (especially salt)

12. All coffees and caffeine teas

Foods that are Alkaline: (DO EAT)

1. All fresh fruits

2. All fresh or steamed vegetables

3. Fresh or steamed mushrooms

4. Corn, whole brown rice, millet, quinoa, buckwheat

5. Potatoes - baked or steamed

6. Olive oil and flaxseed oil (not cooked)

7. Apple cider vinegar, lemon

8. Herbs

9. Herbal non-caffeine teas

10. Distilled water only

11. Dried Fruit

If you are healing a disease, your diet should consist if at least 75% alkaline foods. Eat lots of fresh fruit in the mornings and lots of vegetables (fresh or steamed) in the afternoon and evenings. Try not to eat after nightfall, and try to eat only fruit before noon. Eat moderate amounts. If you decide to do some fasting, never fast too many days in a row. One or two days a week may be good, but do not do them consecutively. If you are healing a form of cancer, do not fast often, this may strengthen the cancer.

If you just want to maintain or improve your health, you should eat 40 to 50% alkaline foods daily. Eat lots of fresh fruit in the mornings and lots of vegetables (fresh or steamed) in the afternoon and evenings. Try not to eat after nightfall, and try to eat only fruit before noon. Eat moderate amounts. Weekly fasting is strongly recommended. Begin with one day per week, and each year or sooner, add another day until you get to 3 days per week. Fasting will not only keep your physical body healthy, but it will also heal and maintain your emotional and mental bodies as well. And, your body will balance to your most natural weight.

If you saw a worm eating your skin you would immediately remove it. Think about it: just because you can't see them does not mean they are not there. Understand too that the manifestation of parasites in the physical body is the direct result of spiritual parasites feeding upon the energy field. Both the physical and spiritual levels must be worked upon simultaneously. To obtain herbal remedies for cleansing, parasite elimination, read the books written by

Michael C. Fikaris

Dr. Clark and Dr. Anderson. I recommend these for everyone.

One last concept: if you have a disease, then give as much as possible. Giving is an essential key to an abundance of health. There was a study by Dr. Alexis Carrol: she studied 140 spontaneous healings (miracles). In the study she asked 200 questions. One question was answered the same by everyone: "What were you thinking at the time you got the healing?" The answer always was "I was praying for someone else to be healed." In order to receive, you must first give.

To truly heal, you must treat the whole human being. All levels must be treated: spiritual, mental, emotional and physical. A change in lifestyle must be manifested. We are living in an artificial reality that promotes sickness, pain and fear. It is up to you to change your world. No one can do for you. Two thousand years ago, Jesus talked about healing, parasites, how to eat and how to be. These truths have been kept from the masses, removed from the scriptures and buried in dust covered basements. But now all things are being revealed. Through guidance, these priceless scriptures have been found and smuggled out for the benefit of us all. Science too is proving what is true and real, but we do not necessarily have the time to wait for science. We must now embrace the truth and fight for our health, happiness and freedom. The intelligence in our bodies has been changed and reprogrammed for sickness. But this intelligence has not been lost and can be reintegrated in an instant. All you need do is to have the courage to stand and be who you are. As Hermes stated:

"Real healing is the integration of mind and body with spirit (consciousness), and knowing that you are One with God (the primal will to Good) and that you are God manifesting yourself as you are. This constitutes real knowledge and leads to wisdom which is the direct experience of this sublime truth. Man/woman is the microcosm, within the macrocosm and as such we truly are gods possessing within ourselves all the powers of consciousness which are inherent within the macrocosm and as such we truly are gods possessing within ourselves all the powers of consciousness which are inherent within the Father/Mother mind."

Chapter Sixteen

REVERSING THE AGING PROCESS
PHYSICAL IMMORTALITY

In every culture in the world, there is the belief that we must all grow old and someday die. And that these things are a part of life that are unavoidable. Of course, this belief is reinforced constantly because everybody we know grows old and eventually dies. So, naturally, in the minds of all humans, this is not just a belief, but a fact of life. Something that must happen to every living creature. Growing old and dying is rarely questioned in the world. But spiritualist have questioned this condition for thousands of years.

We hear stories of Tibetan Monks that have become immortal or have reversed the aging process to the degree in which they stay youthful well into their 80's and 90's. But how do we know that these things are true? All the evidence points to the opposite. We never meet these people. We never see them on television or read any medical research on them. On the other hand, if I were immortal, I would definitely want to keep it a secret from the government and the medical profession. The last thing anyone wants is a bunch of strangers probing every nook and cranny of your body to see why it isn't aging or dying. We do hear about some cultures that live to about 140 years old. One particular group lives in the mountains of Russia and their longevity was attributed to their regular diet of raw honey. The only problem is that these people look like about 1000 years old. Who would want to live that long looking like an old dried up used raisin? Not me, that's for sure!

The question is, "why?". Why do we grow old? Why do we become weak and sick? Why do we die? This is something that the medical profession has been wrestling with for many years. Many doctors have realized many interesting things about the physical body: the body was built to last about 140 years; the body actually heals itself; has the ability to create any chemical known to man; the oldest cells in the body are seven years old; on an atomic level, every atom in the body is changed over every 12 months or so; and they haven't figured out why or how the body ages.

Someday, the medicos will figure out what is going on with the body. In the meantime, we must patiently watch and wait for them to crawl at a snail's pace towards the truth. The problem is that they do not really want the truth, so they ignore reality. And reality is mind and spirit. The spirit is the source of all things in the life of the person and the mind is what creates the health or lack of health of the body. Unfortunately, these things are outside of the perimeters of the scientific world because of their self-imposed structure and limitations regarding research and documentation. In addition, accepting and promoting the truth would interfere greatly with the huge medical industry: everyone from the doctors to the chemical companies. Think about it, there is a lot of money in people believing that they need a doctor or a medicine to heal themselves.

As I stated above, the scientific world has realized that what heals the patient is the patient himself. This has been proven through the tests and experiments with sugar pills. They call this the placebo effect. They have found that if the person believes that the pill will heal then it will. There is a well known story about a man who had cancer: his doctor gave him a medicine and told him that it would cure his cancer, and within three weeks he was healed. Then he read in the paper that his particular medicine does not cure cancer and within a month the cancer was back again. Then a few months later the doctor gave him another medicine to cure the cancer and again the cancer disappeared. But a few months later again he was told that the medicine does not work and soon the cancer returned again and within a few weeks it killed him. There are countless stories like this that demonstrate the power of the mind.

In reversing the aging process, it is important to understand what exactly causes aging. Then to eliminate that cause and replace it with the opposite. I find it interesting how now days people are retaining more of their youth than just 30 years ago. People now in their 40's and 50's look much younger than people did at that age thirty or more years ago. If you doubt this, just look at some old photos of people from those days. Someone thirty-five back then looked like someone 45 or 50 now. How is this possible? Why is it that people are aging differently than in any other time in recorded history? The establishment says that it is because of the excellent health care system, or the quality of life compared to that time period. Well, that could be true in some parts of the world. Possibly in some of the under developed countries. But not so in the western world because in Europe and in Northern America the quality of life has not improved much at all. But the western world is where the change is the most dramatic. So, why is this so? The answer to this is quite simple: people today have a different attitude about aging. People today are not accepting old age as willingly as people in the past. The people today intend to live longer and to stay healthier and more active. Because of this change of mind, the physical body is effected. Thus the power of the mind: a change of mind - a change in body. The body must respond to the

146

mind. Also, this is the trend for the New Age. People will gradually reach that 140 year mark.

Let's talk for a moment about what causes aging. The most powerful thing that causes aging is programming. Deep within the subconscious mind is a strong belief that we must age in a certain way. This programming is passed down from generation to generation. This aging program tells your body to begin to create "older" cells at some point in your life and then to continue creating older cells at a designated pace. This aging process depends on the programming. To identify the programming in your body, begin by examining how your older family members have aged: the physical problems; the diseases; balding; weight problems... etc. Then take a look at how they die: cancer; heart failure ... etc. These things will tell you what to expect if you do not change your programming. Programming comes from parents and other authority figures, such as doctors, teachers, ministers and government officials.

Changing your programming is something that only you can do for yourself. You must learn a system that will enable you to identify all of the aging programming and destroy it or transmute it into a program for youth and vitality. I recommend a self observation meditation that gives needed tools and techniques to transmute these energies. Through deprogramming and reprogramming yourself, you can accomplish anything in the body. The body runs on programming the same way a computer runs on programming. It does what it is told to do according to the programming. The programming exists in the subconscious mind. It is from the subconscious that we create our reality, including the health of the body and the aging process.

147

Michael C. Fikaris

Hypnosis demonstrates this the best. Most people have seen hypnotic demonstrations. A hypnotist can tell a subject that they are as stiff as a board and lay the person across the tops of the backs of two chairs. Then the hypnotist will stand on the person's chest. I personally know a very small woman who was the subject in such a demonstration and she told me that when he was standing on her chest, it felt as if someone was just touching her. And that she felt as if she became a solid board with no effort on her part. The way this works is very simple. The subconscious mind accepts the hypnotist as the authority and will therefore accept whatever the hypnotist says as true. Whatever the subconscious accepts as true and real is what becomes reality in this three dimensional world.

So the first step in reversing the aging process is to change your mind about aging on the conscious and subconscious levels. Decide that you do not have to age in the same way or at the same rate as your family or the rest of the world. But do not only change your mind intellectually, truly believe it is so. Know the truth that this is possible in your physical body and that you must only make the decision. A strong committed decision to live a long, healthy and happy life.

This brings me to the next cause of death: unhappiness and a loss of enthusiasm for life. So many people have no true love for the things that they do in the world. If you are not loving your life, your job, your relationships with people and your circumstances, then life will eat away at you a little at a time until sickness and death are upon you. The word "enthusiasm" comes from the Greek word meaning "God within". When God is truly within and being expressed through you (as it should always be), then your life is lived with enthusiasm. There is an inner joy that welcomes each and every day on this planet. There is a

148

constant love and happiness in all things, no matter how small or seemingly unimportant. Living this way activates the God nature within and continually regenerates the mind and the physical body.

How does one become enthusiastic and happy? Well, that is more simple than most realize. First, you must eliminate all negativity. (Read "Power of the Word"). The next step is to find what it is you love to do more than anything else. This thing should be something productive for society or at least your family - not just eating, sleeping or having sex. Then, little by little, begin to do this thing, and as time goes on, the thing you love will gradually increase in your life until you reach the point where you can derive an income from doing what you love. When you are doing what you love for a living then you are filling your life with enjoyment. Then, work no longer feels negative and draining. Actually, work becomes something that you are enthusiastic about everyday. Soon, you will regret having to take a day off. Understand that at this time in history, you can make money doing anything at all. All you must do is to put your energy into it. Create it in your mind, and take action in the physical world.

What is unfortunate is that so many people grow up. They lose the playfulness of being a child. The reality is that inside all of us is a child. That child of course is the true spirit that you are. But, we have been conditioned to act a certain way in the world, "responsible, mature, serious, sensible, …etc.". So, unnaturally, what happens is that all of this seriousness kills the life and joy within. Suddenly the energy slows down and as the person thinks "older", the body becomes so. This does not mean that we should not learn from life and become better human beings or to be as reckless as a child might be. What I am saying here is that we have a choice. We can have very productive and meaningful lives and still be happy and have fun at the same time! Can you believe it?! It seems crazy, I know, but it is true.

Think about the last time you really had fun doing something. When was the last time you laughed so hard tears streamed down you face? When was the last time you did something really foolish on purpose just for the fun of it? When was the last time you did something you really love to do? When was the last time you felt joy or enthusiasm in your life? If you haven't experienced at least one of these things in the last 72 hours, then you are not living. You are dying and need to make a change for life.

There are many other causes of aging and many more ways to reverse the aging process. These given here, I feel are the most important, plus one other, a daily, in the body meditation practice. Through meditation, you can heal and regenerate on all levels.

It says in the Bible that "to enter the Kingdom of Heaven, you must come as a child". This is true. You are a child. A child of God. Don't deny it. Accept it, be it and live it. The Creator wants to express itself through you at all times. Our only purpose for being here is to learn and to be happy. Growing old is not required, it is a choice that has become unconscious and is now accepted as a fact of life. Why choose to believe in death when we can believe in life?

Every spiritual master that you will ever meet will have this one thing in common: there will always be laughter in the eyes and usually on the lips. They love to play. For us it is important to understand that if we act old, we will grow old. If we act young then we will grow young. Enjoy life! Simple.

Chapter Seventeen

WAR

First of all, let me state that I firmly believe that there are always alternatives to war. The killing of fellow human beings is not only senseless, but further illustrates how truly inhumane the human race is. Living in the United States and especially in the San Francisco Bay Area, one gets the impression that the entire world or at least the population of this country has some inkling of sanity within their consciousness and truly sees the foolishness of war. But, alas, this is not the case. People in the Bay Area, I believe, are very different than much of the world. Does that mean better? No, not necessarily. Just different. "Better" is a judgment that I personally am in no position to make. The concept of "popular war" seems insane to me, but, bottom line is that there has always been war on this planet, and there will continue to be wars for some time to come. And these wars are usually supported by the general population. Even the Vietnam and Gulf wars were "popular wars". The unfortunate fact is, that the vast majority of the world's population are not willing to accept the alternatives to war. At some point in time, one group or country does, by force, accept the alternatives to war, but that is only when that country has been cut down by the sword to the extent that they have no choice - if they wish to survive, they must capitulate with the enemy.

In 1990, we had a situation in the Middle East. Well, there is always a situation in the Middle East! But in that situation the US and the United Nations were more involved in the situation in the Middle East than usual. A situation in which, apparently, no one was willing to accept the alternatives to war. The countries involved were standing upon principles that they believed in strongly enough to sacrifice many human lives, at the very least. The US and it's allies claim that Saddam Hussein was an evil madman who is bent on destroying the free world. George Bush of course was a good and righteous man who was merely coming to the aid of the poor victims of the world who would fall prey to the next apparent Hitler. According to the Iraqis, Saddam Hussein is an extremely religious man (who even makes religious speeches), and the US and George Bush are Satan incarnate who wish to continually take advantage of the Arab Nation, use up their only natural resource and eventually leave them by the wayside to fall into poverty and defenselessness.

The problem with both sides of this propaganda (to use a kinder word), is that nothing could be further from the truth. The reality of what had happened then and what is still happening today will probably not be revealed to the public for many more years to come - if ever. Probably the beginning of World War Three. What did we know about Vietnam in the 60's and 70's? We are just now getting some bits and pieces of information of what really went on during that so-called war. How can anyone in their right mind, for even one minute, believe that the information we receive now is any more accurate, revealing or truthful than what was released in World War II, Korea or Vietnam? Of course, Americans are known for their political stupidity. And our politicians always ensure that the American public remains politically stupid. Do not be upset by that statement. This condition among the American public has been carefully planned and executed for many decades through manipulation of the media and the growing empowerment of the Government over the people. The point here is that most people are being rallied behind wars based upon lies or at best, half-truths. Through manipulation of the media and the economy, the vast majority of the population of most countries are in a constant state of survival, which at the very least, obstructs the individual's ability to see clearly the truth from the lie. And that forces people to support any action which makes them feel safe or at least that something is being done to rectify the situation. One thing that all people understand is that war is good for the economy. Not really a just reason to kill, but justifications can easily be created.

Now, in the year 2002, we are in another situation, not so different than the one discribed above, but much more dangerous. It appears to be different, but in reality, it is not.

Regardless of all the lies and secret motivations and actions of the people in power of the world governments, certain things must happen in the years ahead. All of these leaders - so called representatives of the people - on some level, I am sure, truly believe that what they are doing is correct and is for the benefit of all. I know that George Bush, Saddam Hussein, George W. Bush and Osama Bin Ladin all believed at the time that they are fighting the forces of evil and that the actions they were taking were necessary and unavoidable. I am certain that they all believed that any alternative would be eventual suicide for their own county, religion or principles. Therefore, the only alternative was war. These men were compelled by their own principles, their own reason and their own integrity to do what is correct from their own perspective.

Or were they? Is it a coincidence that two weeks before Iraq invaded Kuwait there was a conference among all the Arab Nations? Or that in the previous year relations between the US and the Arabs and Chinese have been deteriorating rapidly? Or is it a coincidence that the Chinese have been supplying the Arabs with weapons? Or that the US and the Eastern Block countries had suddenly become allies? Or that the US and the Soviets have withdrawn most of their weapons and troops from all of their European bases, leaving the Europeans virtually defenseless? These events could be coincidental, if there were such a thing as coincidence. And, of course JFK was probably killed by a lone assassin. And maybe the government never really did drug experiments on our soldiers. And maybe Roosevelt really didn't know that Pearl Harbor was going to be bombed three days in advance. And possibly Nixon was telling the truth all along. And the CIA never starts any wars or revolutions. And I'll even bet that the government isn't trying to control every breath that you take... Yea, right! The point is, that little war in the Middle East was planned long ago. Things like that don't just happen, especially with the ex-chief of the CIA as President. And the war going on now, (spring 2002, as I edit this section of the book) was also planned and known in advance. How could so many planes be hijacked from the US and no one know until they reached their targets? Imagine the surprise of the people who planned this attack! And, it is no coincidence that Isreal and the PLO are excellerating thier war just at the same time George W. Bush is lumping more nations into the Bin Ladin Terrorist camp...

But, in any event, maybe, just maybe, these world leaders are compelled by a greater power than themselves. Maybe, just maybe, they are not as in control as may be believed. Maybe, although they are manipulating world events to serve their own distorted purposes and ambitions, there is still a greater power in control. That war and the wars to come in the Middle East and throughout Europe and the rest of the world, are necessary. This is just the beginning of a series of events that will have a profound effect upon the world as we have known it. These wars are necessary in order to someday unite the Arab Nations as one and to create a more clear separation between certain nations and to bring together the rest. Why? This planet is going through a cleansing process that has yet to be seen on this planet. A process that will involve wars as well as natural catastrophe. The World is changing and change is not always easy for people. Actually, this change has been going on for some time now. But, the intensity of this process will be increasing rapidly in the coming years. The Gulf war will someday be comparatively considered a minor skirmish. And quite possibly, the beginning of a devastatingly long and costly war. If not the beginning of a much, much larger war. And certainly, these are the events that will set the stage for the wars that I am speaking of.

There is, of course, a time to stand up and fight. We as human beings should not allow ourselves to be controlled or enslaved by anyone outside of ourselves. We must submit to the Creator, which is within us at all times, but we cannot righteously worship false gods from without - or in other words, those who would control us to do their bidding for their own gain or profit. Our own personal freedom is what we should go to battle for at any time and for any length of time. This is worth fighting for and worth dying for. "Put no man before the Lord thy God"; this is the only true freedom. But most people in the world have been conditioned to focus so much outside of themselves that they never consider their own freedom, or the condition of their own lives. So while they campaign and fight and protest and write and worry and cry and demonstrate and litigate and donate for every other person, group or country, their own personal lives spiritually, financially, emotionally and mentally are in a continuous state of decay and degeneration - also known as death.

155

Michael C. Fikaris

Regardless of world events, the only true battle is within. Will you live your life, or will you spend your life dying like the vast majority of the human race? The choice is yours. If you believe that you are a victim, then you will be subject to the circumstances of the world and the people around you. On the other hand, you can take control of your life and thereby create a better life for yourself. But, as history has taught us, freedom has its price. That price is never too great, although it must be paid indeed. The price of true freedom is one must become a true freedom fighter or warrior and thereby conquer the enemy within.

The enemy within can be described as that nature that causes the individual to submit to false gods; to settle for less than what is true and real; to give in to those that will do harm in the name of "love", which is not really love at all; to submit to those who would enslave you throughout life; to not stand upon the principles that you know to be true because of fear of retaliation or ridicule; and the fear to do what is necessary to truly live life to its fullest. These are the things that must be defeated. These are the true enemies. Not the Iraqis, the Bin Ladins or anyone else outside of ourselves. Once these weakness' are conquered, then one may become a Master of his/her life. What are you willing to give up to save your own life or to even have a life? The people of Iraq were willing to die for a piece of land, more than 200,000. What are you willing to do to save your own soul?

In order to survive and to prevail in the 21st century, these are the issues that each individual must address. The wars will come, and many people will die. Where will you be in the year 2020? The answer to that question may be determined by what you do today.

156

Chapter Eighteen

THE VICTIMIZATION OF
THE HUMAN RACE

Interesting title, don't you think? What is it about the word "victim" that is so interesting? I've noticed many times that the biggest news stories are the one's that involve victims. The most popular books and movies are those that involve victims. The most popular causes or passions in the world also involve victims. What is it about victims that moves people? Is it sympathy? Or an overwhelming caring or desire to help others?

People are always moved by victims of circumstance. My whole life, I have felt the pain and agony of people's suffering. In school as a child, when the other kids were humiliating another, I could feel his pain as if it were mine. I would feel more, actually. Often, I wished they would pick on me instead of the other helpless one they had chosen to torture. Somehow, I knew that I could probably deal with it better. Many times, I would step in and help the individual. Many times I was beaten for interfering or standing up to the bullies of the schoolyard. Then, I too became the victim as well. But that was much less pain to bear than the pain of watching someone so helpless be tortured and humiliated.

Now, as an adult, I live in a world of increasingly hideous violence, constant and relentless disasters, and unimaginable pain and suffering. And still, I have compassion for these poor souls that are victims to circumstances. The difference now is in the feeling. I no longer feel their pain and suffering. I am no longer compelled to step in to protect or help, although the desire is

157

Michael C. Fikaris

often present. There are many reasons for this change in character. Not because I have become hardened or jaded. Mostly because I now have a better understanding of what I am seeing in the world and a better understanding of myself.

What I feel and experience now is compassion. What I felt and experienced then was sympathy. There is a big difference between the two. To sympathize is to relate, to share their experience and to identify with them. To only see the surface of the situation without understanding or knowing all of the information. Thereby, making a judgment based upon a limited perspective. Compassion is to understand the person's circumstances, pain or suffering. This understanding comes from experience and knowledge. Knowledge of life and spirituality. This knowledge or understanding gives one a higher perspective, and the ability to see the whole picture. In other words, the ability to see on all levels (physical, mental and spiritual), of what is truly happening and why. When one has this understanding, then the perspective changes. By seeing the entire picture, and by truly understanding what really is happening in any given circumstance, it is not possible to go into sympathy.

People have sympathy in almost all cases with people that are hurt, killed or are suffering in some way. The constant dynamic behind sympathy is that there is a victim. A victim of some sort of circumstance. Without a victim, there is no sympathy. For example, who would you have the most sympathy for: a person who calls himself a stupid shit or the child who's father calls him a stupid shit. Most people, I am sure, would feel for the one that has no control over his circumstances. If you choose to call yourself a stupid shit then you are not a helpless victim. You are choosing your circumstance, and this does not inspire as much sympathy, if any at all. The key ingredient is

158

victimization, and many groups of people fit into this category: the poor, the hungry, the homeless, the children, the sick, the handicapped, the insane, the minorities, the third world countries, the gays, the abused, the senior citizens, the Jews, and often even the women... and of course, the list is endless.

Today, there are more special interest groups then ever before. Everyone now days, who see themselves as different, feels that they need some sort of special treatment, benefits or help. They feel this way because they feel that they have been victimized. Being a victim in today's world is always accepted and most of the time almost glamorous. Tragedies become big news stories, then novels and then movies. The worse the tragedy the more rich and famous the person becomes. Victims have become the heroes. People today walk around wearing their past suffering like a badge of honor and an identity bracelet. They compare and measure each other by the size of their emotional scars rather than actual achievements. And everyone today seems to have some emotional scar that they carry like a cross to bear. To me, this is like a disease. We call it "Poor-little-me-itis".

This condition seems harmless on the surface. But I must tell you that this condition is deadly. Deadly because this cross becomes a block, an excuse, and an emotional barrier to life. Seeing one's self as a victim is the single most dis-empowering state of consciousness a person can possess. And seeing others as victims is almost as bad. Let me explain...

What most people do not understand is that everything that happens in life is for learning purposes. This planet is nothing more than a schoolhouse for human beings. This is a pure and simple truth. Your sole purpose for being here is to learn the spiritual laws, to learn about life and most importantly, to learn about yourself: who you are; what your true nature is; what your first loves are (what do you love to do… etc.); what your talents are; what your mission is on this planet; what your strengths and weaknesses are and how to transmute those weaknesses into strengths and how to express your strengths more consistently; and to discover what it is you are to do in the spirit world when you graduate from this school. Because of this fact, everything that happens to you, (good or bad) is designed specifically to teach you something that will fall within one of the above categories. These lessons are constant and endless. As long as you have a body, you have something to learn.

Therefore, it is important to take responsibility for your life now as it is, and for everything that has ever happened to you throughout your life on this planet. You must realize that there are not and never were any accidents or coincidences. And you must realize that you were never a helpless person or a victim of circumstances. That you not only agreed to everything that has happened to you, but that you helped to create those experiences. The reason this is so crucially important is simple: As long as you shift the responsibility to another person or a circumstance, you have shifted your power away from yourself. This loss of power erases your ability to learn from the experience. If you have the perspective that these experiences are for your good, than you will investigate and discover the value of the lesson at hand. In addition, you will then realize how, as a spirit, you created the circumstances for the experience. Thus bringing you a better understanding of how you as a spirit creates in this world. Understanding that will bring to you not only the needed information from the lesson, but will also bring to you more power as a spirit in a body (which you are!).

Now here is where you are probably asking "What about the little babies who do not know what is happening to them?" And that is where I say "What makes you think they do not know what is happening?" Babies are far more aware than people realize. Just because they haven't learned to communicate like the rest of us yet, does not mean they do not know what is going on around them. Remember, we are talking about spiritual beings. Until the age of 14 years, children are guided and protected, and given only the experiences and lessons that are important for their development on this planet as human beings. Everything that happens on this planet is done by spiritual agreement. Everything! No exceptions. Many of you might say "Well, I never agreed to be so abused as child", or "I never agreed to contract this disease". Yes you did. You just are not conscious of your spiritual agreements yet. But someday you will be. Not only did you agree for these things, but your energy and actions created the experience.

Everything comes through the law of Cause and Effect. Everything has a direct and traceable cause. The agreement is just part of your creations, your actions are what manifests your agreements. So anyone can look at any situation and see clearly how they caused it. These actions can be physical, mental or emotional. Physical actions are obvious. The mental and emotional are not so obvious, therefore the person must do some intensive inner study to see these causes. But know that they are there and as it says in the Bible "Seek and ye shall find". This takes courage, focus and a strong desire to be free.

Another cause is simply by allowing the experiences to take place. For example, someone is walking down the street in Los Angeles and suddenly there is a gang war gun fight and this person gets caught in the middle of it and is shot. What action did he take to cause this? It could have

161

Michael C. Fikaris

been many, such as: fear and an obsessive worry of being shot, a negative perspective and belief about surviving, or possibly other actions on an emotional or mental level. Or, through allowing it to happen. Maybe he agreed for this to happen for learning purposes, so his action was to put his body at that place, at that exact time and then to do whatever is necessary to get shot exactly as agreed upon. This too applies to babies. As spirits, they have chosen their parents and situation on Earth. They make sure that they are in the right places at the right times, they inherit the physical limitations that are needed for their lessons.

Where I live and work in Berkeley, California, there are a great number of handicapped people. Literally hundreds right near our Institute because one block away is a center for the handicapped. Consequently, I've had the opportunity to get to know some people who are blind or in wheelchairs. The one common thing that I have learned is that they really do not want or need our sympathy or to be treated like victims. They all respect me because I treat them like anyone else. I see them as healed and whole and somehow this makes them feel better. But this is just on one level. Spiritually, when you see someone else as a victim or powerless, you are feeding their weakness rather than their strength. It says in the Bible, "Where two agree, there I am." This is a spiritual law. When two people agree upon anything, then it can manifest. Think about your past conversations with people when someone was feeling victimized... Notice how the more people the victimized person can get to agree that they are a victim, the more of a victim they become. When someone is feeling or seeing themselves as a victim and you also see them as a victim, then together you quadruple that power in the negative or make them that much more handicapped, whether it be physically, mentally or emotionally.

162

In addition to this, there is another spiritual truth to consider: "What you see, what you think and what you say, is what you create". Seeing, thinking and speaking are actions. If you see people and yourself as victims, then you will create that reality for yourself through your own belief and through the energy created through thoughts and words. (Read "Power of the Word"). Therefore, it is important to completely erase your belief in victimism altogether. It is too dangerous for yourself and for others, even deadly.

Through the media, victimism is constantly being promoted. People are now on talk shows everywhere crying about their past tragedies, seeking sympathy, recognition, validation and money. Parents are instilling in their children the same sick and demonic attitudes by being over protective and shifting blame for everything to everyone else. Weak and irresponsible parents will create, raise and nurture weak and irresponsible children. Every time a child hears a parent say "I can't" then the child can't either. Parents create the limitations in their children through demonstration. Something in human nature wants to pass down not only what is good and strong but also what is weak. People have the need to explain themselves to their children, and most of the time this means playing the victim game so that the child will not see the truth. The truth being that the parent is weak and unwilling to do what is necessary to create a productive and meaningful life. And all of this is supported by the psychologist, the government and of course the media. These people want you to be weak, victimized and dysfunctional creatures. That way you will need their services and need to hide in the illusion that you are being taken care of, soothed and nurtured by them. The human race has been systematically transformed into a big blob of helpless humanity that is more and more dependent upon social services rather than individual abilities.

163

Michael C. Fikaris

The fastest way to heal yourself is to first admit that you are responsible for your entire life. Then look to see why you created certain lessons. Once you can do this, your life will change for the better. Never being a victim again is a big step for the great majority of people, because hardly anyone now days wants to take responsibility for their hardships - only for the good things. Few will want to admit that they have created such a mess in their lives, or have repeated the same blunders over and over and over again. It is easier to put the blame upon someone or something else. Thereby appearing spotless in the eyes of others. But there is no power in this game and this promotes continual hardships. We say "If you act like a victim then you will become one, but if you act like the Master of your life and destiny, then you will be." You cannot have it both ways, you must choose one or the other. It is only a decision away.

Try to imagine a spiritual Master whining about his or her past or present conditions. You have now come to a fork in the road. You will choose one path or the other: the path of the worldly way, weakness and blame that leads to death; or the path of responsibility, power and self mastery, which leads to life eternal. A difficult choice. The right one requires strength, perseverance, persistence and patience. I pray that you make the courageous choice, give up victimism and thrive through life.

Chapter Nineteen

THE EVOLUTIONARY PROCESS

How do we evolve? We evolve through learning. So, how do we learn? There are as many ways to learn as there are people in the world. Everyone has his or her own individual path in life, and life is about learning. Therefore, everyone learns in his or her own individual way. If you are a student of spirituality, and if you truly study spirit in all ways on all levels, then you have probably already discovered the truth that there is only one true spiritual teaching. Or really, one true spiritual understanding. This spiritual truth is and has been expressed in countless ways throughout history through many masters, teachers, prophets, writers and a host of people from all walks of life. The basis of all the great religions, including the New Age teachings, is exactly the same, based upon the same principles of spiritual truth, and the laws that govern the Universe. But these basic spiritual revelations are expressed in many different ways in order to reach people who exist on many different levels of consciousness.

The teachings of the Masters have been repeated for hundreds or even thousands of years. Yet, people are just now beginning to accept and understand the inner meanings of what was said. This is merely the first step to true enlightenment. The first level of understanding is recognition of what is true. If one is aware, when he hears the truth, it is immediately recognized on a conscious level. For many people, this recognition is unconscious and does not become conscious until it is heard many times. At the point of recognition of a spiritual truth, or the validity of a

Michael C. Fikaris

spiritual law, a door is opened for understanding to manifest within the individual's consciousness. Understanding is not necessary for recognition or acceptance. Within everyone is a mechanism that enables us to recognize what is true. Acceptance is a matter of will. Often, recognition and acceptance is manifested through faith: faith in the teacher or in the source of information.

Understanding comes through deeper study, observation or thought. Many do not take this step. Actually, most in the past have not taken this step. This time in history is unique in that many are suddenly beginning to understand what is recognized. Understanding brings clarity to what is recognized. This understanding offers the possibility of increased personal power. It does not guarantee anything, but it opens the door to realization, which will bring actual power.

Where we are today as a race of humans is right here at this level. Millions, maybe even billions of people are beginning to understand the spiritual information that has been given for so long. This is a revolutionary step for this planet, but still very much a beginning step in our spiritual evolution. Most people that obtain spiritual understanding will not take the next step to realization of that understanding during this lifetime. The understanding will remain on an intellectual level where it can never be utilized for the benefit of the individual or for those around him. In most cases, the understanding without realization is a dangerous state to be in. As it is said, a little knowledge is dangerous. This is true; knowledge can empower or do the opposite, depending upon how or if it is used. To know the truth and to not live the truth is like playing Russian roulette. Eventually, whatever you are consciously denying through your actions, or lack of action, will destroy you. This is where integrity becomes an issue.

The next step is realization of what is understood. Realization is the act of integrating what is understood into your life. This is a conscious act. At this level, the individual is moving what is intellectually understood into his everyday thoughts, words, perceptions and actions. Whatever the person does is in harmony with what he spiritually knows and understands to be true. At this point, the person does nothing that is in conflict with his understanding of truth. This action empowers the individual to create consciously the life he was intended to create, and more importantly, it will allow him to become himself as a Son or Daughter or God – a true representative of the Universe. Through this self-realization, the door is opened for the next step in the learning/evolutionary process.

This next step is the expression of Light. The good and the true now flow naturally through the individual for the world to see and to learn from. The information is now fine-tuned to the point where the individual sees God in all things. He realizes that there is no separation, that there is nothing in reality but the Light and that all things are of that Light. The person now is compelled to demonstrate the simple truth of the Universe in whatever ways are offered. During this level, God-realization occurs. There no longer is any doubt that you are a part of God, and so is everyone else. The true nature of God is present in all aspects of life, and this truth is not only realized, it is always consciously expressed.

The next level of learning is creation. Consciously creating as one with the Creator. Few have ever reached this level during his or her life on Earth.

So, who are you really? People run around today proclaiming "I am a child of God!" We hear it all the time, and throughout this book that same statement is repeated in many different ways. But, what does this really mean? What are we really saying?

For many, it is easy to accept that we are children of God. That of course makes us Sons and Daughters of God... This fact is a bit more difficult for most to swallow. But really we are just touching the surface here.

Forever, (almost), people have been programmed to believe, think and act as if we were just an extension of the animal kingdom, like talking monkeys. Our true divinity has been systematically hidden, denied, lied about, or perverted in many different ways. The Masters of this world and the spiritual realms have been presented to us as much different then we are. Although there were many, we know of only a few authentic Masters that have incarnated here. Most of these Masters have been through trials and tribulations that the rest of us could not really relate to in practical terms. We've heard little of the many female Masters that have incarnated. Most were hidden from world or were quickly executed.

Some, like Jesus, were said to have been conceived differently than the rest of us. Yet, he never said that... In fact, it was not the Masters that put themselves "above" us, or made themselves different than us. It was their followers. A true follower follows. Unfortunately, these "followers" didn't follow, they took over. They worked their way in and changed things. Most people in the world now are following these false profits, or "replacement" masters. In other words, they are following the followers of the Masters, rather than the Masters. They are learning interpretations of truth, rather than the pure truth that was originally given. They are receiving false light, like sitting under a light bulb rather than in the sun.

So, to actually reach our true goal, our soul purpose for being on this planet, we must look to the Light of what is real and true. That Light exists within us at all times. We must agressively reject those that mean to confuse and mislead us. We must vigously transmute all the lies that have been embedded within our conscousness for Thousands of years, and finally accept who we truly are.

Who are we then? What does a child of God grow up to be? What does a child of a bird grow up to be? A child of an elephant? A child of a snake? Your own children? It is so obvious, isn't it? "Our Father, Who art in Heaven..." How could Jesus be the "only begotten Son of God"?? He never said that! In fact, if anything, he said the opposite. He never made those separations, nor have the other Masters. We are no less God than anyone or anything else in this Universe. And, we are no more God than anyone or anything else. That is the reality of this Universe.

So, when do you grow up? Or, maybe more relevent, when do you *want* to grow up? That is really the issue. At some point, if not already, you will be inspired to be who you truly are. When that happens, nothing will stop you, because you will realize beyond any doubt that *you* are the only person that can stop you.

In order to achieve these levels, much is required. Because of the programming and hypnosis of the human race, spiritual truth must be repeated and reinforced countless times before the steps begin to be taken. The words of the Masters are always repeated over and over again so that they can be understood on deeper levels. Spiritual knowledge is expressed in thousands of ways and demonstrated continuously to open the eyes and ears of those that are ready to see and to hear. The levels of sleep and darkness must be broken so that the Light can flood in. This can happen through extreme experiences or through repetition.

To take these steps in learning, one must give up the belief that there are conflicting spiritual truths. One must stop the intellectual masturbation and begin to live the truth. Spirituality is not about knowledge; it is about transformation, becoming yourself in the highest sense. It is about doing, taking steps and continually moving forward. That is the purpose of knowledge: to create and express all aspects of life in the Light.

Chapter Twenty

JOY

There are 7 basic emotional levels that we deal with most of the time. These levels are:

> Joy
> Enthusiasm
> Amusement
> Anger
> Boredom
> Apathy
> Death

Death is the emotion that should be avoided at all costs. If you reach the emotional state of death then you have gone too far in the wrong direction, unless it is truly time for your transition. But death can be experienced in the physical body way before the actual death of the body. Just look around within your own family or circle of friends, you will surely see someone that is not really living, but merely existing. This is someone who has no original thoughts, has no fun or enjoyment in life, just repeats everyday the same as the last, and has no hopes or dreams or desires left in his or her consciousness.

Apathy is a little better. A person can still have a desire or two in life, even the hope of a distant dream. But this emotion brings mostly hopelessness and depression into the present. Although the person is still alive, it is hard to tell. They are immobilized physically and spiritually starved.

Michael C. Fikaris

They have spent the energy within them - whatever was good - without replacing that energy. They are like a car that has run out of gas, abandoned on the roadside, waiting for someone to come along with a gas can to get them going again.

Boredom is something that many people experience for various reasons. Mainly because they won't open their eyes to see the world and what the world has to offer. The truth is that if you are bored, then you are missing all the things that can be enjoyed in life - you are missing the abundant opportunities to live an exciting and fulfilling life.

Anger is the best of the negative emotions, because although anger can be destructive outwardly and inwardly, it can also heal. If used consciously for the purpose of healing, then it can purify. But, unfortunately, that is rare. It takes a conscious human being to control and utilize the healing power of anger. Most of the time, anger is the result of frustration or some past time experiences that has created underlying resentments and hatred. Usually self-hatred is at the base of it, although self-hatred is mostly unrecognized. Self-hatred is always projected outwardly towards others. This is because of the spiritual law to "Do unto others as you would have them do unto you". What this really means is that we always treat others as we treat ourselves. If you selfishly deny yourself of quality thoughts and positive energies, then you will be selfish with others as well. If you are hateful and angry with yourself, then you will be that way towards others too.

It is said that "you are never upset for reason you think". This is true. Whenever you are experiencing a lower emotion, it is important to go deeper within and become conscious of what really has triggered that emotion. Just begin by asking "why". "Why am I upset? Because John called me a shithead. Why does that bother me? Because it isn't nice. So what. Why do I care? Because my childhood friend Bill used to call me a shithead. Why did that bother me? Because I wanted to be liked. Why? Because I was insecure. Why? Because my father didn't appreciate who I was. Why does that still upset me now, what did I need to learn from that? I need to be more aware of my divine nature and more excepting of who I am. Why do I need to learn that? Because I am basically judgemental. Why am I judgemental? Because my whole family is. What do I need to learn from that? That everyone is perfect just the way they were created. And? And we are all God's children. And? And so am I!" In this way, it is possible to get to the bottom of what is upsetting in your life. Usually, people are emotional about just one or two things that need to be healed or resolved within. When that happens, they become happy again, as are most children.

Amusement, enthusiasm and joy are our natural states. Amusement is the lowest emotion we should experience (unless we are purposely using anger to heal, then we can express anger. But even then, we are still at least amused and even enthused or joyful about what we are doing). Amusement requires vision. Not 20-20 eyesight, but spiritual vision. The ability to see what is truly happening within and around us. When this vision is developed, one begins to gain an understanding of reality, and through this understanding, it is difficult to be upset. The reason for this is that the individual sees that God is truly in control and that all things are for learning. And that learning is our true and only purpose for being on this planet. This vision also enables the person to realize that what happens in life is by agreement and that we create our own reality and our own experiences. And most of what is created on this earth is illusion designed to give us our learning lessons. And the joke is, that we believe that this shit is real. Having this consciousness and understanding on a real level insures that you will never dip below amusement.

Once this is established, then true enthusiasm begins to grow. Enthusiasm for life. The word enthusiasm originally meant, or came from a Greek word meaning "God within". Many people mistake excitement for enthusiasm. The difference is simple. Enthusiasm never goes away. Excitement is short lived, and comes and goes. Excitement brings with it emotional highs and lows, enthusiasm brings a consistent building of energy, so once a high is reached, it is maintained. Enthusiasm is God expressing him/herself through the human form. Enthusiasm is nourished by a true love for the Creator, creation and life.

The ultimate emotion is Joy. Joy is linked with Freedom and Life. To be in the state of Joy is to be in heaven. It is to be in Love with Life and all of creation. It is a state of truly living life without death. Death and Joy cannot exist in the same place at the same time, (unless death is purposely and consciously being used for transmutation). And with Joy is always a sense of Freedom. Like truth, Joy can set you free. The reason for this is that the only reality is in truth and in joy. And the truth is joyful, because the truth will reveal to you who you are, and the reality of the universe. This knowledge of truth engenders freedom and a true and divine love for life. This knowledge makes you as one with the Creator, or, in other words, allows the Creator to be you, consciously.

Do you think that the Creator, our God, is depressed? Angry? Bored? Apathetic? Jealous? Resentful? Vengeful? Hateful?... Of course not! What kind of a God would that be?! Not a God I would follow! I wouldn't even follow a

Teacher with these attributes. Would you? I hope not! But if you are expressing these lower emotions, it is not possible for the Creator to express Him/Herself through you. Why? Because you are not allowing God in. You are closing the door with negativity. Does this mean that God does not have the power to come into you if God wanted to? No. This means that you have free will at all times to express whatever you want to express: good, bad or ugly. This is how you allow God to be you. You elevate your consciousness beyond the lower emotional levels that block God out.

Think for a moment, when in the past you experienced the emotion of Joy. Think of how your life was going at that time. You were probably in love. There was no fear, no failure, no disease, no depression or any of the lower emotions, people didn't effect you so negatively... In short, you were empowered. You were open to a piece of the Creator. Some of that nature took a hold of you and life was like magic. Flowing easily and joyfully.

There is so little Joy in the world today. Rarely is Joy expressed even in the movies or television. But there are a few people on the planet today filled with Joy. And most, I dare to say, are on a spiritual path. A path that has led them out of the darkness into the Light. But even the majority of people that are on a spiritual path today, walk with a burden on their shoulders, stern looks on their faces, seriousness in their speech, severity in their eyes and anger in their hearts. These people haven't found the Joy of spiritual growth. They find evil in laughter and in dance. They still believe in a punishing and angry God. And to them, holy means suffering. There is nothing further from the truth. Jesus said "I bring you good news". GOOD news! Not suffering! Not punishment! Not seriousness!

175

Michael C. Fikaris

As you walk along the path of light, rejoice! Laugh at your creations. Laugh at the ridiculousness of human consciousness. Laugh with each and every lesson and watch how much better your life becomes. Never, never give up on your hopes and dreams and always, always be amused! The path to God, Light, Life, Freedom and Joy are all one and the same. How can you make it through seriousness, anger, hatred, boredom, apathy or death? Where is it written that these are the ways to eternal life? Jesus said "I am the Truth, the Way and the Life". Where did He demonstrate these negative qualities? He even defied death to prove He was for real. So, what have you done to prove you are for real? Are you for real? Have you at least gotten past boredom or apathy?

There is an AA (Alcoholics Anonymous) saying: "Fake it until you make it". Try it. Express Joy, Love, Enthusiasm or at least amusement and it will become a reality for you. Your true nature will always be expressed. Have fun, for Christ's sake. Have fun for your own sake so the Christ can join with you. Why do Angels fly? Because they take themselves lightly. Do you?

Chapter Twenty-one

PROSPERITY

Thus far, in this book, I have given to you many of the necessary tools to acquire the health, wealth and abundance that anyone would desire. Read and understand these chapters on an inner level and then put these concepts and spiritual laws into practice. This action, combined with practicing your meditations will enable you to prosper in all areas of life. Practicing some of these concepts and not all of them will most likely result in some form of lack. Everything that was presented to you here must be used to the extent that it becomes part of your everyday life. I recommend that you reread the chapters often according to your needs. Each time you do, you will receive new realizations and clean out deeper levels of programming, negativity and lack. If you find it difficult to stay on the path or if you find that you wish to continue on in your training, then I invite you to consider the Spiritual Development Program offered by the Institute for Spiritual Development. The following is another important spiritual law.

When I was fourteen years old, I decided that I was going to be wealthy. People would ask me what I wanted to be when I grew up and I would reply simply, "Very wealthy". Then they would ask what I wanted to do to become wealthy, and I would reply simply, "Anything". As far as I was concerned, the end justified the means. I even considered professions such as gigolo, assassin and even practicing law! In my quest for wealth, I worked in over thirty-two different jobs. I practically supported myself

Michael C. Fikaris

from the time I was twelve years old and helped to support my mother, stepfather, brother and two sisters from seventeen until I was twenty-eight years old. At fifteen, I began studying psychology and prosperity. I read everything I could get my hands on concerning both. I went through intensive money/wealth workshops regularly and training programs from fifteen years old and on. By the time I was twenty-seven years old, I owned four businesses, a condo, a new Cadillac, lived in a $600,000.00 home in the Peacock Gap area of San Rafael and had $125,000.00 in the bank. Most of this success was due to my spiritual training. When I started my training I was struggling like everyone else. One year later I had manifested the above material gains and retired from the world of the 98%-ers.

What are 98%-ers, you might ask. Well, the 98%-ers are the vast majority of sleepers in the world. The people that live mediocre lives, never really tasting life at all. Just rethinking the same old thoughts and going out of their way to make sure that they fit in with the rest of the world. These are the ones that never ever take a risk. The ones that are really old inside before they are thirty. These are the people that are dying through life rather than really living physically, mentally, emotionally or spiritually. They always know what to think, but rarely how to think. These are the robots of the world, the slaves, the walking dead, the zombies, the blind, the weak and the fearful. This is what I walked away from in 1981. This "secure" comfort zone - more like the twilight zone to me.

Since that time, my life has been simply learning and teaching spiritual truths. In 1984, I walked totally away from all of my material wealth and began teaching. I have prospered and have always been able to maintain my lifestyle as a student and teacher of spiritual truths. I must give credit where credit is due: I did nothing but constantly

178

surrender to Universal Law. I gave up my life and it was saved; and then I was given the life that I truly wanted. I practiced faithfully and consistently the techniques and concepts that were taught to me and that I have taught to you in this book, plus one other.

In all my training and in all my experience, the one most constant and important spiritual principle that was repeated to me from the age of fifteen years old was TITHING. Now is when most people cringe and roll their eyes back. It took me eleven years, until I was twenty-six years old to hear this message. I always assumed it was some sort of scam created by the Churches and "prosperity gurus" to get their hands on MY money. So I never believed in tithing. Then when I met my Teacher, who trained me one-on-one, I began tithing. I gave freely, with no strings attached, to the source of my spiritual food - my Teacher. Consequently, I began to prosper. The more I prospered, the more I gave. In three and one half years, I gave over $60,000. Yet, at that point, I did not totally understand what tithing was. I just really liked to give. In retrospect, a couple of years later, I realized that the times I stopped giving, my prosperity faltered and when I gave with strings it was as if I never gave at all. So, I began to study the laws of giving and tithing.

Spiritual law states first, that as a spiritual teacher I must teach the laws of tithing. If I do not, then I am withholding information that will effect the life and well being of the student. So I am obligated to give to you the following information.

The word "tithe" comes from the word tenth. Ten percent of everything that you receive in any way, shape or form belongs to God. In other words, you must give away ten percent of your GROSS income, gifts or whatever. This tithe must be given to wherever you receive your spiritual food. Your teacher or your church. Tithes must be given freely without expectations or strings. In other words, what is done with the tithe is none of your business because it does not belong to you anyway. Remember, it belongs to God. Also, do not give to get. Giving in expectations of receiving is not giving - it is buying. There are three tithes: each is a 10% increment. Ten percent is the minimum that must be given back to God in one way or another. To really get the full benefit of tithing, then tithe 20% of your income, plus an annual tithe. The first 10% is your basic tithe, the second 10% would be for charity and the annual tithe consist of a tithe to wherever you receive you spiritual food most of the time, given once a year in January. This tithe is amount equal to one week's income. Most people work their way up to these amounts. But if you just tithe 10%, believe me, your life is going to change for the better. Understand that God does not need you to give, it is you that needs to give back a portion of the abundance that you receive.

To truly win at the money game, one must understand that money is energy. It is programmed by you as soon as you touch it with your conscious awareness and understanding of its correct use and purpose. Philanthropy is one of the highest levels of being. The true purpose of wealth is to give. Whether that wealth is in the form of money, knowledge, energy or material objects, the more you give away to those that can have, the more you will receive as a channel. Remember that you can not out give the Giver. Whatever you give FREELY will surely return to you ten fold. And what you withhold of God's, will surely be taken away - plus ten fold.

Use this information wisely. Regardless of your path, it applies to all at all times. Every course and workshop I took in prosperity from the age of fifteen stressed tithing. Each

180

person must have the freedom to do and live according to the guidance from the God of their own Heart. So whatever you do is between you and the Supreme Being. I have fulfilled my obligation as Teacher. Now you know the Law, now you have the Knowledge.

Michael C. Fikaris

THE CHRIST POEM

I have walked the Master's path into the Light
And along the way, I too, have lost my sight.
I have journeyed within the depths of hell
And faced the darkness we all know so well.

The road back was so long… so painful,
Until I opened up and beared my soul.
The demons I thought were tearing my life apart,
Were really Angels helping me to free my heart.

And as the Angels cut the pain away,
I dreamed of peace and solitude someday.
To be alone in my loneliness…
To be at one with His Holiness.

The dream of all dreams for me, the Son
Must come after the work that I Love is done.
But now I must speak to you who are here,
So listen now with your golden ear.

As I've traveled through Love and Life,
I've been many times beneath the surgeon's knife.
Cutting and slicing, a bit at a time,
Until what was left was soulfully mine.

If you look deeply and clearly into my eyes,
You may somehow learn, to know, to realize
The dimensions and the levels that I have seen,
And to know, in truth, what that vision means.

Look a little closer, do you see the pain? The misery?
Just look at me! Go ahead... Look into me!
I have seen it, I have lived it, and I have healed,
But your fate has not yet been sealed.

You must choose your path, and begin the fight,
To love only what is good, and of the Light.
For you must learn to walk again,
In Love and Light and Joy again.

So few will learn,
So few return,
From the misery of pain,
From the hopelessness of blame.

Yet, before you I stand,
With open, spotless hands.
Longing to see the Light in your face,
Filled once more with joy and grace.

You must learn, and you must return,
From the pain and the misery,
To Life, to Love, to me,
For I Am that I Am
And I Am for you!

Michael C. Fikaris

ABOUT THE FOUNDATION FOR
SPIRITUAL FREEDOM

The Foundation for Spiritual Freedom was founded in Berkeley California in 1984 by Michael C. Fikaris. The purpose of the foundation and it's institutes is to help individuals become truly free through the self realization process. It is our belief that within each person is the power to be free and independent from all people, places and situations. We know that the only true possession in life is the freedom to express one's true self and that our entire lifetime here on planet earth is for that attainment. Our goal is for each individual to become their own teacher, healer, psychic, minister and counsellor.

ABOUT THE AUTHOR

Michael C. Fikaris was born right in the middle of the USA. He was raised from the age of seven in San Francisco, California. Michael consciously talked with spirits and angels during his childhood until the age of fourteen. At that time, he thought he must be crazy, so then began studies in psychology, self hypnosis and self-improvement courses.

Throughout childhood he was exposed to spirituality through the Catholic school system and the Greek Orthodox Church. Because of obvious contradictions in these religious systems, his hunger for spiritual understanding was not satisfied during those early years. After reading countless books, including the Bible, Michael focused his attention on building a successful business. For about five years Michael put spirituality in the back of his mind.

In 1981, at the age of twenty-six, Michael met who was to become his most important spiritual Teacher. This was a dramatically life-changing event. The first thing Michael learned was that he was not crazy at all. Michael's Teacher, Bill Duby, spent countless hours daily, for more than forty intensive months, guiding, teaching and training Michael in all aspects of spirituality, meditation, healing and clairvoyance. Michael also worked under the direction of three other spiritual Teachers over a period of many years.

In December of 1984, Michael founded the Foundation for Spiritual Freedom. Since that time, he has been lecturing, counseling, and training people throughout the world to become their own teachers, healers, and counselors. He has reached thousands of people in one way or another through his centers, articles, lectures, television and radio. His understanding is that all people have within themselves all that is needed to heal themselves on all levels and to create a healthy, happy and prosperous life right here and now.

Made in the USA
San Bernardino, CA
20 February 2013